Lupercalia

Lupercalia
Rites and Mysteries of Wolf Worship
Author: Alberta Mildred Franklin

Cover image: *Romulus and Remus* (detail) Peter Paul Rubens 1615/1616
Illustrations: Rijksmuseum Amsterdam
Lay-out: www.burokd.nl

ISBN 978-94-92355-31-7

© 2017 Revised illustrated publication by:

VAMzzz Publishing
P.O. Box 3340
1001 AC Amsterdam
The Netherlands
www.vamzzz.com
contactvamzzz@gmail.com

LUPERCALIA
Rites and Mysteries
of Wolf Worship

Alberta Mildred Franklin

VAMzzz PUBLISHING

contents

CHAPTER I   Introduction — 9

New knowledge about the religion of the Mediterranean race offers
a new basis for a study of the Lupercalia. The characteristic deity of
the Mediterranean race was an earth-goddess, incarnate in all natural
objects, the giver of life and of death, and worshipped by orgiastic rites.
The characteristic deity of the Aryans was a sky-god, who was honored
by a calm, rationalistic ceremonial.

CHAPTER II   The Ceremonial of The Lupercalia — 29

The ceremonial rites of the Lupercalia were complex and seemingly
incoherent. The Romans had vague ideas about the presiding god, but
regarded the purpose of the festival as (a) protection from evil, (b)
productivity, and (c) purification.

CHAPTER III   The Wolf-Deity in Greece — 33

The wolf-deity of the Greeks was Pelasgian; he represented the
devouring power of the underworld, and was worshipped by rites of
expiation.

CHAPTER IV   The Wolf-Deity in Italy — 45

The wolf-deities of Italy, among them Lupercus, were also dreaded
chthonic powers, and had cults of the Mediterranean type. The
Lupercalia originated among the Ligurians, and at first consisted of
the sacrifice of a goat to Lupercus, a ceremonial tasting of the entrails,
an expiatory flight by the priests, and a feast. It was an apotropaic
ceremony designed to ward off evil.

CHAPTER V   The Sacred Goat in Greece — *73*

The goat-god of the Greeks was a Pelasgian fertility god. His fertilizing power was often appropriated by anthropomorphic gods.

CHAPTER VI   The Sacred Goat in Italy — *81*

In Italy the goat-god was also the giver of fertility, and originated among the Ligurians. Juno was closely associated with the goat, and some of her fertility rites were added by the Romans to the Lupercalia: the Luperci girded themselves with goat-skins and, as they ran about the Palatine, struck the women with goat-skin thongs as a fertility charm. Henceforth the gift of fertility was one of the important purposes of the Lupercalia.

CHAPTER VII   The Dog as Sacred Animal in Greece — *103*

The dog-cults in Greece were Pelasgian, mainly of Thracian origin; and had especial potency for purification.

CHAPTER VIII   The Dog as a Sacred Animal in Italy — *113*

The dog-cults of the Italians seem to have been borrowed from the Greeks of Southern Italy and Sicily. The Sabines, who adopted many Mediterranean customs, who were familiar with the purificatory power of the dog, and who exerted a powerful influence over the religion of Rome, probably added the sacrifice of a dog to the Lupercalia. Thus purification came to be an important element of the Lupercalia.

CHAPTER IX   The Blood-Ceremony of The Lupercalia — *125*

The blood-ceremonial of the Lupercalia finds no parallel in Roman cults, but is similar to certain rites of the Orphics which sought to assure complete union with the deity. It is probable that these Orphic elements were added to the Lupercalia during the war with Hannibal, or the years immediately following, when many orgiastic cults of the Greeks were brought into Rome. Thus the Lupercalia was spiritualized by new rites of cleansing and by the assurance of kinship with the deity.

CHAPTER X   Resume — *143*

In its development the Lupercalia reflected the development of the Roman people.

Bibliography — *147*

Post Scriptum

CHAPTER I

Introduction

WITHIN THE LAST few decades the work of the archaeologist and of the anthropologist, revealing the civilization that existed thousands of years ago, has brought about a revolution in the study of Ancient History. Before this time scholars who dealt with the history, the social life, and the religion of Greece and of Italy were concerned preeminently with the Aryan peoples who invaded those peninsulas. The earlier stock was largely disregarded, as being merely the aborigines who had been effaced by the conquering Hellenes and Italians. The falsity of this view has been abundantly demonstrated by the discovery of the marvellous civilization of Crete and of Mycenae. Surely a people so numerous, so powerful, and so cultured are to be reckoned with, if one would understand the later populace of those lands. The Neolithic inhabitants of Italy too, though far more primitive than those of the Aegean, were possessed of a civilization too clearly marked to be ignored.

In religion more than in any other realm the influence of these pre-Aryan peoples is of vital significance: The sanctity attaching to religious beliefs and ritual makes them peculiarly resistant to change.

The deity of a certain locality is supreme in his limited realm, and his cult must in many cases be received, either wholly or in part, by the new-comers. Consequently the divine objects of worship and the ritualistic acts of the pre-Aryans have been of late years increasingly emphasized in investigations dealing with the religion of Greece or of Italy.[1]

This new method of approach arouses a hope that it may lead to a solution of some of the puzzling practices of Roman ritual. Perhaps the most interesting and the most perplexing of all the Roman festivals is the Lupercalia, with its incoherent and fantastic ceremonial, its prehistoric origin, and the varied accounts of it. Consequently, though the Lupercalia has been a subject of speculation since Varro's day, it is worth while, now that we have a new point of departure, to try once more to solve the riddle.

Ethnologists are very generally agreed that the Palaeolithic Age in Europe was terminated by the appearance of a new race, known as the Mediterranean or Eur-African. In physique the people of this race were uniformly dolichocephalic, of medium height, and of slight build. At the time of their appearance in Europe they had attained a considerable degree of civilization, using implements of polished stone, and showing a strong tendency to an agricultural, non-nomadic life. They had developed definite and elaborate funerary rites: the dead were buried, often in a carefully constructed tomb, and were surrounded by the implements which they had used when they were alive. This practice argues a belief in a future life in which the dead continue to exist in the grave, keeping the same needs and interests which they had on earth. This Mediterranean stock gradually spread until it had occupied Mesopotamia, the Mediterranean basin, Western Europe, the British Isles and the lowland portions of Central Europe as far east as the upper Danube.[2] It has been characterized as the most widely extended, the most populous, and the most primitive of European races.[3] For the present study our interest must be centered in the branches of the Mediterranean race that settled in the Aegean area and in Italy. To designate these, two ancient terms have been restored to use. The branch that occupied the lands which later formed Hellas are known by most ethnologists as Pelasgians, the one occupying Italy as Ligurians.[4] Along the Mediterranean the ease of communication united with the racial kinship of the people to produce a highly developed and homogeneous civilization. From the oldest culture centers of Egypt and Crete, civilization radiated to the kindred, but less advanced, peoples of Asia Minor, Greece, Thrace, the Danube area,[5] Italy, Sicily, and Spain. Thus there developed in the peoples dwelling near the Mediterranean a similarity of culture which is recognized by all authorities.[6]

By the beginning of the Bronze Age another ethnic group, generally known as Aryans, Indo-Europeans, Alpines, or Eur-Asiatics, had occupied the Alpine belt which extends through Europe and Asia. They are generally believed to have had skulls of brachy cephalic form and larger frames than those of the Mediterraneans. Their language was Indo-European. From very early times they cremated their dead, usually burying with the ashes little or no funeral furniture.[7] This practice is usually interpreted as indicating a belief that the soul, upon death, was separated from the body and departed to a remote realm, severed from all contact with the living.[8] The Alpine people were far more inclined to a nomadic pastoral life than were the Mediterraneans.[9] Very early, it seems, bands of Aryans began straying into Greece, though, according to most views, their influence did not become marked until the latter part of the Bronze Age. Then during several centuries, down to the beginning of the Iron Age, a series of Aryan tribes overran Greece, Thrace, the Aegean Islands, and the coasts of Asia Minor.[10] Italy, whose development was later than that of Greece, had just entered upon the Bronze Age when a branch of the Alpines migrated to the Po valley, and there established numerous settlements which are known as *terremare*. Toward the end of the Bronze Age bands of them moved southward, and one group settled in Latium. At a later period the Umbro-Sabellians, who had been long separated from them,[11] occupied the Apennines and the neighboring valleys.[12]

From the fusion of the Mediterranean populace with the invading Aryans arose the Greeks and the Italians of historical times. In such a fusion the race that has, through many centuries of habitation, become adjusted to a region is almost sure to show the greater vitality and, in the end, to absorb the intruding race.[13] Thus, in the case of the Greeks and the Italians, though the mixed peoples adopted the Indo-European language, they soon reverted to the physical type of the Mediterraneans. Even today the southern Italians are the physical counterpart of the people who inhabited Italy before the Aryan invasion.[14] In culture and in religion, as well as in physical type, the Mediterraneans, who vastly outnumbered the immigrants, must have had a very great influence in the development of the united peoples.

For our earliest picture of the religion of the Mediterranean race, we turn to the remains of Minoan Crete and of Mycenae. There we see that the chief object of worship among the Pelasgians was a goddess, who was evidently an earth-deity. Often associated with her was a youthful male, who seems, at least in some instances, to have been a sky-god. He always appears as a subordinate; the goddess was the all-important divine being. She was embodied in human form, and frequently had a lion, a dove, a snake, or some other animal in attendance. Numerous representations of monstrous figures, part human, part animal, probably portray the lesser *numina* of woods and waters. Fetish objects of especial sanctity were stones, pillars, trees, animals of many kinds, and weapons, such as the hield or the double-headed axe. These cult-objects typified sometimes the varied productive power of the earth, sometimes man's means of defense against his enemies. In primitive times they were probably regarded as incarnations of the deity. Later, when the goddess was fully anthropomorphized, they became her emblems or her attendant animals. The deity was not worshipped in a temple, but upon a mountain, in a forest, beside a spring, or, most frequently of all, in a cave. At her shrine men offered sacrifices of animals or of fruits. Figures of men clad in animal-skins, which frequently appear on gems or on seals, are often taken as representing the worshippers, who are showing honor to the deity by wearing the skin of her sacred animal. The dead too, were objects of worship, and elaborate ritual acts were performed at their tombs.[15]

This Pelasgian goddess is believed to have been closely similar in character and functions to the Cretan Rhea, to the Phrygian

Cybele, to many forms of the Greek Artemis, and to various other deities of the Aegean area.[16] Each of these later deities typifies the life-giving power of the earth. Every living thing, whether it be a plant, an animal, or a human being, derives its existence from her. She likewise takes them back to herself at the end of life. This goddess is no departmental deity, but has power over every activity of man or of the universe. Each manifestation of nature is sacred to her or is her very embodiment. Thus she may be adored as incarnate in the stone, the tree, the lion, or the goat, her particular form in each locality being determined by the physical features of that place and the character of the people inhabiting it. The sphere of action of the goddess is intensely local, her power and manifestations in each region being inseparably attached to some definite place. She is the goddess of love, and is constantly associated with a lover or a son, as Attis, Adonis, or Dionysus.[17] To him the bull is especially sacred. This male god is not immortal, but shares the seasonal changes of vege-tation, dying in the fall and reviving to new life in the spring. These occasions are celebrated by the worshippers with extravagant orgies of mourning and of joy. In the death and the resurrection of the deity the people find assurance of human immortality. Much of the homage offered by this agricultural people to its earth-goddess consists of fertility charms to arouse the dormant powers of productivity or to secure rain for the crops. But often, for some inscrutable reason, the goddess withholds her blessings, and sends barrenness, blight, and pestilence upon her people. To avert these destructive forces and to set free all beneficent activities, the devotees resort to strange orgiastic practices. Often they seek to propitiate the dread goddess by the sacrifice of a human being.[18] Frequently the ill-will of the deity is attributed, to some sin committed by man. Therefore rites of cleansing are of vital importance. Often man seeks guidance from oracles, through which the earth-deity speaks to her people. The earth-goddess, who nourishes the living, also receives the dead. They continue to live on in the tomb, and are, if duly honored, the kindly protectors of their descendants; but, if angered, they become merciless demons, and must be "averted" by ceremonies of riddance. Often the more distinguished dead develop into local *heroes* and are honored by cult-acts similar to those performed to chthonic deities. This worship of earth-goddess and of local divinities, while it is a religion of fear, and is expressed in barbarous and magic rites, has in it the lofty elements of dependence upon the deity, of the sense of impurity, and of the possibility of cleansing and of communion with the god.[19] Sir Arthur Evans says of this chthonic religion that it is characteristically non-Hellenic, having nothing to do with the traditions of primitive Aryan religion.[20]

An equally detailed picture of the religious beliefs of the pre historic Aryans is, unfortunately, impossible. When the Aryans migrated from their primitive home they went to lands which, in most cases, were already occupied. A racial modification of the Aryans must, accordingly, have begun in the very earliest times.[21] Concerning the original religion of the Aryans, who were already a mixed race when they appeared upon the stage of history, we can draw only general conclusions based upon philology and upon the religious beliefs which were common to the oldest Aryan peoples. Most authorities agree that the sky, with its varied manifestations, was the supreme object of worship among all primitive peoples who spoke the Indo-European language.[22] The sky was early embodied in a god who was called "the father," as "father Zeus," or "Jupiter." There was, perhaps, the conception of the earth as mother, the wife of the sky-god, but her importance was slight compared to that of her spouse. There was, therefore, an emphasis exactly opposite to that of the Mediterranean religion, in which the earth-mother was supreme, and the sky-god her subordinate.[23]

For the oldest literary picture of the religion of the Hellenes we turn to the Homeric Poems. These cannot be accepted as a portrayal of a purely Aryan religion, for Homer's Achaeans,who had been in Greece for many years, perhaps for several centuries, had adopted much of the civilization of the Pelasgians, and must also have been influenced by Pelasgian cults. But, even so, they had a slighter admixture of Pelasgian blood and ideas than had the Greeks who appear in any of the later literature. Therefore it is reasonable to attribute to Aryan influence the Achaean religious beliefs and cults which are markedly different from those of the Pelasgians, especially if such beliefs and cults are to be found among other Aryan peoples when at about the same stage of development. The religion which is portrayed in the Homeric Poems is pre-eminently rational, with only an occasional suggestion of mysticism. Instead of a chthonic deity and a host of vague and nameless *numina,* the Achaeans worshipped anthropomorphic gods who lived in palaces on Mount Olympus, and were organized into an orderly commonwealth with Zeus, the god of the sky, at their head. These deities were highly specialized, each one having some definite province and function of his own.[24]

They had none of the mystery which attached to the Mediterranean gods, but were strongly individual and human, having the might of gods, but all the wicked passions of mortals.[25] Men treated them like human beings, sometimes upbraiding them, or even making sport of them, as is done in the story told by Demodocus about Ares and Aphrodite.[26] The Achaean gods were not, like the Pelasgian, limited in their power to some special spot; they were the gods of the tribe rather than of the place. In their ritual acts Homer's people did not perform mysterious or orgiastic ceremonies, nor did they resort to magic to secure the growth of crops or the increase of their herds; instead, they prayed to the gods and offered sacrifice in decorous fashion.[27] Those acts duly performed, man's whole duty to the gods was done. He had in their presence no consciousness of sin or of the need of cleansing. If he had committed a murder, he was not required to atone to the gods, unless the injured man were, like the priest Chryses,[28] especially dear to one of them, but he paid a fine to the nearest kinsman of his victim. When he had thus made reparation, he did not need to be purified, as in later times, by the sprinkling of blood, nor did he fear the pursuit of a vengeful ghost. The dread of demons and the worship of heroes is, indeed, almost unknown in the Homeric Poems. When the body of a man had been consumed upon the funeral pyre, his soul was believed to depart to Hades, where he lived a vague shadow existence, remote from the activities of the living. Libations were offered as a part of the burial ceremonies, but there was no cult attached to the grave, as there was to the tombs of Pelasgian *heroes.*[29]

In comparison with the Mediterranean religion, the religion of the Homeric Poems was rationalistic instead of occult, a worship of calmness instead of ecstasy, a homage paid to immortal, anthropomorphic, specialized gods with a sky-god as their chief, instead of to gods who were mortal, of shifting, often of theriomorphic form, among whom an earth-mother was the supreme deity.

In the religion of classic Greece these two strains seem to have united. There are, on the one hand, the Olympian gods and the state ritual substantially as they are portrayed in Homer. But along with them are many cult-practices which are attested by archaeology and by literature [30] that correspond to Pelasgian instead of to Homeric religion. The rite of inhumation, which seemed almost unknown in Homer, has again become common. The Homeric indifference to chthonic deities and to mysticism has disappeared, and the worship of gods of the earth and the performance of magic rites of the most primitive kind is widespread. The homage paid to the Brauronian Artemis, the sanctity attaching to the Eleusinian Mysteries, and the human sacrifice offered to Zeus Lycaeus, all seem far removed from the sanity of the Olympian religion. Not only in remote places like Arcadia did these relics of savage belief persist, but they found a strong hold even in intellectual Athens. Orphism, which took as its chief deity Dionysus, a god having all the characteristics of a nature-spirit of the Mediterraneans, and which derived its ritual acts from the most primitive practices of Crete, developed a theology that was the loftiest expression of Mediterranean creeds. This Orphic theology profoundly influenced some of the greatest minds of Greece.[31]

It seems an anomaly that a people which, in about the ninth century before Christ, was almost free from occultism, witchcraft, and hero worship, should afterward revert to the beliefs of a remote past. The natural and the generally accepted explanation is found in the dual origin of the Greeks, composed, as they were, of Pelasgians and of Aryans.[32] The assumption that the presence in Greek religion of chthonic deities and of chthonic cults is due to the Pelasgian strain of the populace seems almost inescapable in view of the fact that these cults were most marked in the places that had the smallest infusion of Aryan blood. These regions were Crete, whose Pelasgian civilization was too deep-rooted to be effaced by the invaders;[33] Arcadia, whose people were regarded as the most typically Pelasgian of any Greek populace, and whose cults, the most primitive in all Greece, show a close affinity to those of Minoan Crete;[34] Attica, whose Pelasgian stock was less adulterated than that of any other land of continental Greece except Arcadia;[35] Boeotia, which was influenced more deeply by Crete than by the Aryans;[36] Lycia, which in prehistoric times seems to have been closely connected with the Cretans, and which remained dominantly Mediterranean in race and cults;[37] and the Ionians of Asia Minor, who had the largest infusion of Pelasgian blood of any Hellenic stock.[38] In all these lands the religion was strongly chthonic.[39] From these facts Andrew Lang concludes that the Achaeans imported a new, lofty, and *brief-lived* set of ideas and customs.[40]

In the union of the two religions, compromises of every kind were effected. Frequently the local god was absorbed by, or was regarded as identical with, one of the Olympian deities. Under this influence, the Pelasgian cult was often purged of its wild excesses and its cruel rites. On the other hand, the Mediterranean god frequently changed his name, but not his character, and continued to receive the same primitive homage as before. Often the animal in whom the earth-god was incarnated became attached to the Aryan god. This god appears at times, therefore, in guise of the animal, or attended by it. Often this animal is the most acceptable sacrifice that can be offered to the god. In every possible manner the new ideas are seen mingled with the old.

In the religion of the Romans it is vastly harder than in the religion of the Greeks to disentangle Mediterranean beliefs from Aryan creeds. There was no Italian Homer to portray the religious ideas of the Latins or of the Umbrians. The dominant position of Rome tended to smooth down the local differences in religious practice which are often a valuable guide in Greek religion. Archaeology tells us, however, that before the invasion of the Aryans every part of Italy was occupied by the Ligurians, whose civilization was in the essentials markedly similar to that of the Pelasgians,[41] and had been, indeed, to some extent inspired by them.[42] Traders and, perhaps, colonists from the lands of the Pelasgians caused the Neolithic civilization of Southern Italy and of Sicily to become more closely associated with Crete and the Aegean world than with Northern Italy.[43]

When the Ligurians were overrun by the Aryans, a mixture of race and of culture similar to the mixture which we have observed in Greece seems to have occurred in Italy. In many localities of Italy are found inhumation-tombs and cremation-urns belonging to the same period.[44] In this fusion the *terramara* folk could hardly have failed to be profoundly influenced by the earlier inhabitants of the land. Professor Pinza holds that the civilization of Latium borrowed from the Stone Age its rites, its technical processes, its habitations, its tomb architecture, and its artistic taste.[45] Professor Modestov goes so far as to say that we might consider the population as not Latin at all, except for a certain number of incineration graves. He regards it, therefore, as wholly natural that the Latins and the Romans had in their religious beliefs been deeply influenced by the Ligurians.[46]

In the religion of historical Rome are found two strains that are similar to those of Greek religion. There were, on the one hand, the sky-god Jupiter and the other gods of the state cult, who, until they fell under Greek influence, were little more than highly specialized abstractions, their power and nature being defined instantly by their names. The *Indigitamenta* of the Romans offer one of the best examples of the *Sondergotter* of the Aryans. The religious ceremonial of the Romans was orderly and unimaginative, similar in its type to the Homeric cults. On the other hand, there were chthonic deities, whose origin was lost in antiquity, and whose ritual consisted largely of fertility charms and magic rites. There were many cult-survivals that recall the characteristic features of the Mediterranean religion. Veneration of springs, trees, and sacred animals was widespread, and ceremonies to avert evil and to secure purification were common.[47]

This dual strain in Roman religion seems most naturally inter preted by an analogy with the religion of Hellas. In Italy and in Greece the basic stock was Mediterranean, the subdivisions that settled in the two peninsulas being closely related. In both Greece and Italy the Aryan invaders showed the same skeletal structure, followed the same practice of cremation, spoke kindred dialects of the Indo-European language,[48] and worshipped a sky-god called by the same name. In each land archaeology proves that a fusion of races took place. In Greece the honor given to earth-deities seems almost inevitably traceable to the Pelasgians. Consequently the parallel conclusion for Rome seems reasonable.[49] The Romans themselves felt that chthonic gods were alien to them, for they constantly remarked on the affinity of such deities to some earth god of the Greeks, or, in many cases, held them to be a Pelasgian importation.[50] Furthermore, the localization of many of the chthonic cults of Italy gives cause for connecting them with the ancient inhabitants of the land. If a cult is strongly associated with some prominent natural object, such as a mountain, a river, a cave, a spring, or a tree, we have a strong reason for believing that it was a product of the race that had been longest established in that place. Later invaders find the spirits of these places exalted by a homage that has been developing for centuries. Inevitably they desire to secure the favor of these gods of their new abiding place, and so they accept the established cult. Mr. Gomme says: "Let us once clearly understand that the local fetishism to be found in Aryan countries simply represents the undying faiths of the older race".[51]

In the present study of the Lupercalia, the attempt will be made to learn the origin of its various cult-features by comparing them with similar cults or beliefs among the Romans and the Greeks. In this investigation the localization of a cult - that is, the people by whom it was first practised, and its association with some natural feature of the country - is a point to be kept constantly in mind. Moreover, far more illumination is to be obtained from Greek reli-

gion than from Roman. The individuality of the Greek states offers
in many cases a reasonable degree of certainty for discrimination
between the cults of the Aryans and those of the Pelasgians. When,
therefore, we find a cult in Greece that is Pelasgian, and a similar cult
of Italy which has been from ancient times closely attached to some
prominent object of the landscape, and which was by the Romans
themselves assigned to a non-Roman populace, the logical conclusion is that the Italian cult belonged to the religion of the Ligurians.

In the study of a subject like the Lupercalia, one cannot hope
to arrive at an incontrovertible conclusion. The antiquity of the festival and the scanty evidence concerning certain parts of it preclude
so ambitious a hope. We must, consequently, be content with the
modest aim of establishing a reasonable theory.

NOTES
*(The first time a book is cited, the title is given in full; after that, an abbreviation is used.
O.M. refers to the original manuscript in 1921.)*
1. This point is stressed by Sir Arthur Evans, *Minoan and Mycenaean Element in Hellenic
   Life*, in *J.H.S.* vol. xxxii, 1912, 277. See also Schrader, *Die Indogermanen*, 132, 153; id.
   Prehistoric Antiquities of the Aryan Peoples, iv; Farnell, in *The Year's Work in Classical
   Studies*,1908171; Lang, *The World of Homer*, 2.
2. For the the orks about the Mediterranean race, see Sergi, *The Mediterranean Race*, 30-
   40, 247-65; Ripley, *The Races of Europe*, 461-70; Keane, *The World's Peoples*, 307-12; id.
   Man, Past and Present, 446-54; Taylor, *The Origin of the Aryans*, 54--{i9, 92-101; Myres,
   The Dawn of History, 39-43; Meyer, *Geschichte des Altertums*, i. 2. 809-34; Hawes, *Crete,
   The Forerunner of Greece*, 22-5, 144-6 ; Mackenzie, *Myths of Crete and Pre-Hellenic
   Europe*, 57-8, 164; Peet, *The Stone and Bronze Ages in Italy*, 111, 163-77; Modestov,
   Introductiona l'histoire romaine, 110-13
3. Ripley, 451; Keane, *W. P.*, 312; Grant, *The Passing of the Great Race,*149.
4. These terms, as used by modern authorities, include all the pre-Aryans (See Schrader,
   Aryan Religion, in Hastings, *Ency. Rel.*, vol. i, 35; Hall, *The Oldest Civilization of Greece*,
   83-4). Thus Minyae, Leleges, Carians, Eteocretans,and other less important groups
   are now all known as Pelasgians; while Siculi, Ausonians, and others are grouped

together as Ligurians.

5. Some authorities prefer to regard the civilization in the Danube area as an independent northern development. See J. Hampel, *Neuere Studien uber die Kupferzeit*, in *Zeitschr. fur Eth.*, vol. xxviii, 1896, 57-91.

6. Sergi, 275; Ripley, 130; Hall, *The Ancient History of the Near East*, 5; Mosso, *The Daum of Mediterranean Civilization*, 62. For the characteristics of Mediterranean civilization, see Hall, *Aegean Archaeology*, 44-254; id. *O. C. G.*,83-104; id. *N. E.*, 56-61; Hogarth, *Authority and Archaeology, Sacred and Profane*, 228- 42; Mackenzie, *Crete*, 191-292; Burrows, *The Discoveries in Crete*, 197-201; Hawes, 27-45, *et passim;* Sergi, 266-315; Myres, *D. H.*, 42; Beloch, *Griechische Geschichte*, i. 1. 71-3, 96-125; Meyer, i.2. 762-94; Keane, *M. P. P.* 462-8, 528-30; Grant, 153-5; Worsaae, *The Prehistory of the North,*19-23.

7. Ripley, 470-5; Keane, *W. P.*, 355-6; id. *M. P. P.*, 501-6; Beddoe, *The Anthropological History of Europe*, 15; Sergi, _ 237-46; 263-5; Taylor, *69-92;* Peet, 370; Mackenzie, *Crete*, 151; Kretschmer, *Einleitung in die Geschichle der griechischen Sprache*, 59-75.

8. Hogarth, *Auth. and Arch.*, 247; Chadwick, *The Heroic Age*, 422, 425; Schrader, *Ar. Rel.*, in Hastings, *Ency. Rel.*, ii, 30; Mackenzie, *Crete*, xlvii; Rohde, *Psyche, Seelencult und Unsterblichkeitsglaube der Griechen,*i,249.

9. Beloch, i. l. So; Taylor, 89, 164-5; Mackenzie, *Crete*, 151,233.

10. Hall, *O. C. G.*, 104; Hawes, *25-6;* Burrows, *201-2;* Keane, *M. P. P.*, 532-4; Meyer, i. 2. 804-8, 815-34; Cotterill, *Ancient Greece*, 28, 34-6.

11. Modestov, 239-40.

12. Munro, *Palaeolithic Man and the Terramara Settlements in Europe*, 338-45, 413-29; Modestov, 103, 143-285; Peet, 331-71, 396-9; Piganiol, *Essai sur les origines de Rome*, 15-22; Sergi, 176-9; Keane, *M.P. P.*, 528-9. Dr. Beddoe (129) says that the Aryan waves of immigration largely spent themselves in the north.

13. Ripley, 30-3; Taylor, 198-203; Mackenzie, *Crete,*146-7.

14. Ripley, 269-72; Evans, *J. H. S.*, vol. xxxii,287.

15. Evans, *Mycenaean Tree and Pillar Cult*, in *J. H. S.*, vol. xxi, 1901, 99-204; Hogarth, *Aegean Religion*, in Hastings, *Ency. Rel.*, i, 141-8; Dussaud, *Les Civilisations prehelleniques, 327-413;* Hall, *A.A.*, 145-77; id. O.C.G., 293-302; Tsountas and Manatt, *Mycenaean Age*, 294-302; Graillot, *Le Culte de Cybele*, 1-41 Burrows, 112-14, 127; Mackenzie, *Crete*, xliv-xlvii, 59-6o, 159-62, 293-312; Hawes, 139-43; Reinach, *Orpheus*, 76-8; Meyer, i. 2. 789; Beloch, i. 1. 110-13; Cotterill, 48-56; Kretschmer, 194-5.

16. Evans, *Scripta Minoa*, 291; Farnell, *The cults of the Greek States*, iii,1-2, *291- 2 ;* Hall, *N. E.*, 52; Dr. Mackenzie *(Crete*, 61-9, *Myths of Babylonia and Assyria*, 101-4) notes that this Pelasgian goddess was also akin to the great earth deities of Babylonia, Egypt, Germany, and the British Isles. See also Graillot, 5.

17. Although Dionysus seems to have originated as an Aryan deity (Beloch,i. l. 1651 n. 1), he is believed to have absorbed very early, under Pelasgian influence, the characteristics of an earth-god (Hall, *N. E.*, 476; Farnell, *Natural and Comparative Religion*, 18; Beloch, i. l. 165; Dussaud, 392; Campbell, *Religion in Greek Literature*, 269).

18. The existence of human sacrifice in Crete has not been proven by the excavations (Hogarth, *Aeg. Rel.*, in Hastings, *Ency. Rel.* , i, 146), though it may be echoed in the

legend of the victims offered to the Minotaur *(Harrison, Prolegomena to the Study of Greek Religion,* 482; Cotterill, 56; Piganiol, 99). In Arcadia, Attica, and other territories in which the populace was dominantly Mediterranean, both cult and legend give numerous proofs of the practice of human sacrifice. Dr. Westermarck *(The Origin and Development of the Moral Ideas,* i, 443-54) notes that it is especially frequent in agricultural rites. See also Mackenzie, *Bab.,-* 104; Farnell, iii, 93.

19. For a description of the chthonic cults of the Aegean peoples, see Evans, *J. H. S.,* vol. xxxii, *279- 80 ;* Meyer, i. 2. 705-33; Hall, *O. C. G.,* 293-302; Dussaud, 385-93; Graillot, 7-24; Murray, *Four Stages of Greek Religion,* 15-53; Rohde, i, 204-15; 249-50; Lippert, *Allgemeine Geschichte des Priestertums,* ii, 503; Tsountas and Manatt, 302-12; Mackenzie, *Crete,* 69-72, 153-8, 165-90; id. *Bab.,* 81-101; Lawson, *Modern Greek Folklore and Ancient Greek Religion,* 529, 536-9, 562-9, 576-90; Cotterill, 44, 48-57; Myres, *D. H.,* 186-7; Dieterich, *Mutter Erde,* IO, 84, *et passim;* Farnell, iii, 1-28, 289-305; Harrison, 8-31, *et passim.*

20. *J. H. S.,* vol. xxxii, 280.

21. Schrader, *Indoger.,* 132; id. *Ar. Rel.,* in Hastings, *Ency. Rei.,* ii,36.

22. Schrader, *Indoger.,* 141, 143; id. *Ar. Rei.,* in Hastings, *Ency. Rei.,* ii, 15, 33; Meyer, i. *2.* 867; Beloch, i. 1. 152.

23. For a survey of the religion of the primitive Aryans, see Schrader, *Indoger. ,* 132- 49; id. *Ar. Rei.,* in Hastings, *Ency. Rel.,* ii, 30- 8, *et passim;* Meyer, i. 2.867-73, 915; Beloch, i. l. 150-65. It is usually held that the sky-god appeared in this early period in the form of a tree or of an animal. But the proof of that statement rests upon the forms of the sky-god seen in later times, after the Aryans had, in their various new dwelling places, mingled with the older inhabitants. For example, Schrader, to prove that Zeus was embodied in a tree or in an animal, cites Zeus of Dodona and Zeus Lycaeus *(Ar. Rei.,* in Hastings, *Ency. Rei.,* ii. 45,37-8). But Dodona was, according to all ancient traditions, Pelasgian (Hom. *Jl.,* 233; Herod. *2.* 52), and is so accepted by modern scholars (Graillot, 7; Campbell, 38; Cotterill, 58); and Zeus Lycaeus, as we shall see later (See pp. 21-4) was a Pelasgic deity with whom Zeus had no kinship either in character or cult. Meyer (i. 2. 915) says that there is scarcely a trace of *Baumkultus,* nor yet of acult of actual animals, among the Aryans. Dr. Beloch (i. l. 152) believes that various animal epithets of Hellenic deities, such as Βοῶπις Ἥρη, or Γλαυκῶπις Ἀθήνη, go back, at least in part, to the Mycenaean Age. It seems safer, therefore, to make no attempt to visualize the deities worshipped by the ancient Aryans.

24. This tendency to departmental gods, or *Sondergotter,* as they are calledby Dr. Usener *(Götternamen,* 75), is accepted as one of the most characteristic features of Aryan religion (Schrader, *Ar. Rel.,* in Hastings, *Ency. Rei.,* ii, 32 ;Usener,122.

25. Dr. Farnell *(N . C. R.,* 13) says:"Of the Hellenic religion no feature is so salient as its anthropomorphism." He believes that the lack of mystic qualities of the Hellenic gods was due to their anthropomorphic form, saying *(N.C.R.,* 16) that theriomorphism lends itself to mysticism because of the need of seeing something back of the crude animal form; whereas the Olympian deities could seem nothing else than glorified human beings.

26. Hom., *Odys.*, 8. 266- 366.

27. The sacrifices offered to the gods were regularly domestic animals. The only time that a human being was sacrificed was at the funeral of Patroclus (Hom., *Il.*, 23. 23) and that was not an offering to the gods (Lang, *Homer and his Age,* 95-6).

28. Hom., *Il.*, i. 10-1r.

29. For the religion of the Achaeans, see Adam, *The Religious Teachers of Greece,* 21-67; Campbell, 56-83; Lang, *W. H.,* 132-4, 266-7; Leaf, *Homer and History,* 11-23; Murray, 57-99; Rohde, i, 9-32, 43-8, 97, 126, 271 n. 3; Chadwick, 415-26; Cotterill, 45-7; Lawson , 521-2, 529-30.

30. These two strains are noted by Isocrates *(Or.,* 5. 117). Occultism, hero worship, fear of ghosts, magic, and rites of purification are mentioned very frequently by Hesiod, the Cyclic Poets, Pindar, and the tragic writers, especially Aeschylus (Lang, *H. A.,* 20; id. *W. H.,* 2, 150; Campbell, 108-9, 173, 278-80, 283-4). For the evidence of archaeology, see Harrison, 166-82, *et passim.*

31. For these two strains in Greek religion, see Reinach, *Orpheus,* 78--91; Rohde, i, 200- 2; Campbell, 127-36, 238-66; Tsountas and Manatt, 313-14;· Cotterill, 43; Lang, *W. H.,* I 17; Gruppe, *Griechische Mythologie und Religions geschichte,* 48-50, 58-61, 101-4, *et passim;* Farnell, i, 261-2, iv, 1-8, 112-13, *et passim;* Harrison, 1-7, 363-453, 473-511, *et passim.*

32. Hogarth, *Auth. and Arch.,* 243; Hall, *A. A.,* 85; id. *N. E.,* 520; Leaf, 261-83; Beloch, i. 1. 92, 150; Evans, *New Archaeological Lights on the Origin of Civilization in Europe,* in *Smithsonian Institute Annual Report,* 1917, 444; Myres, *D. H.,* 216. Mr. Lawson has traced in modern Greek religion many survivals of Pelasgian religion (79-98, 43-44, *et passim),* and shows (5-52) that these elements had a far more vital hold upon the people than had the Olympian deities. The same survival of pre-Aryan elements has been noted in the religion of India. Dr. Keane *(Aborigines,* in Hastings, *Ency. Rel.,* i, 35) states that the Aryan deities of that land are all of the sky, that they are on a kindly and familiar footing with their worshippers, and have no gross or cruel forms of worship; whereas the chthonic deities of the Aborigines must be appeased by blood. In the union of the two races, it is stated, these latter gods largely replaced the heaven-gods of the Aryans.

33. Hall, *O. C. G.,* 203.

34. Farnell, ii, 620, v, 9; Hall, *N. E.,* 59; id. *O. C. G.,* 82; Evans, *J. H. S.,* vol. xxxii, 283; Graillot, 7.

35. Hall, *O. C. G.,* 203; Lang, *W. H.,* 141; Meyer, i. 2. 769; Fick, *Vor-griechische Ortsnamen,* 129; Grant, 160.

36. Hall, *N. E.,* 59; Gruppe, 59-61; Fick, 99.

37. Hall, *N. E.,* 6o n. i; id. *O. C. G.,* 87--91; Kretschmer, 372-6; Fick, 125.

38. Hall, *N. E.,* 67, 79; Lang, W. H., 143-g; Grant,16o.

39. Lang, *W. H.,* 157-6o; Evans, *J. H. S.,* vol. xxxii, 277-87; Hall, *O. C. G.,* 203-8; Campbell, 37-42, 238-42; Beloch, i. l. 144-76; Meyer, i. 2. 724-34; Burrows, n4-16; Cotterill, 31, 78-80.

40. *W. H.,* 153.

41. Modestov, 252, 254, *et passim.*

42. Montelius, *Die vorklassische Chronologie Italiens,* 149-56; Keane, *M. P. P.,* 530;

d'Arbois, *Les premiers habitants del'Europe,* i,129; Mackenzie, *Crete,* 247-8. 43.

43. Peet, 86,143, 284; Myres, *D. H.,* 221.

44. Myres, *D. H.,* 233.

45. Pinza, *Bullettino delta commissione archeologica comunale di Roma,*1900, 201.

46. Modestov, 254. See also Sergi, 179, 244; Taylor, 204; Reinach, *Orpheus,* 95; Myres, *D. H.,* 231.

47. Dr. Piganiol (93-143) notes many such cult-practices among the Romans.

48. Kretschmer,154.

49. Though Dr. Warde Fowler avoids discriminating between Mediterranean and Aryan cults, he devotes two chapters of *The Religious Experience of the Roman People* (24-67) to what he calls "survivals." In discussing them, he frequently says of some quaint or magical act that it seems un-Roman, or that it may have been taken over from an earlier people. He makes this statement about the Lupercalia (ibid. 34; *Roman Festivals,* 312). Dr. Lippert (ii, 545) assigns all the cults of the mother-goddess to the pre-Romans, and those in honor of *Divus Pater* to the Romans. Dr. Piganiol (93-143, *et passim)* makes a similar distinction, tracing all chthonic cults to Mediterranean inspiration.

50. See page 57. In the following citations, Roman cults are said to be similar to Greek cults, or are derived from them: Saturn, Serv. ad Verg., *Aen.,* 8. 319; Faliscan Juno, Dionys., I. 21. 2; Juno Sospita, Ovid, *Fast.,* 2. 55; the rite of the Argei, Fest.,334.

51. *Ethnology in Folklore,* 71. Professor Rhys, in his study of Celtic religion, discriminates in this way between the greater divinities of the Aryan pantheon and the numerous *genii locorum* of the pre-Aryan inhabitants *(Celtic Heathendom,* 54, 105).

CHAPTER II

The Ceremonial of The Lupercalia

AT THE OUTSET of our study of the Lupercalia we need a clear picture of the ceremonial acts. Though the Lupercalia was very frequently mentioned by ancient writers, Plutarch alone gives all the details of the ritual. His portrayal, therefore, will serve as a general survey.

"The Lupercalia," says Plutarch, [1] "from the time of its celebra tion, might seem to be a ceremony of purification, for it is performed in the ill-omened days of the month of February, a period which an-yone would interpret as devoted to expiation; furthermore the very day of the Lupercalia was in olden times called *The Purification.* But the name of this festival is the same as *Lycaea* in Greek, and for this reason it seems to be a very ancient festival of the Arcadian immigrants who followed Evander. But this is merely the general explanation, for the name may in fact have been derived from the she-wolf [of the Romulus legend]. And, indeed, we believe that the Luperci begin their race about the city at the spot where, they tell us, Romulus was exposed. The ceremonial, however, makes the origin of the rite hard to guess. For goats are slain, then two boys of noble rank are led up to the victim, and a sword which has been dipped into blood is pressed upon their foreheads, after which the blood is immediately wiped off with a bit of wool moistened in milk. The blood having been removed, the lads must laugh. After this [the Luperci] cut the hides of the goats into strips and, naked except for a girdle, they run about [the Palatine], striking with the thongs everyone whom they meet. The young women do not shun the blows, since they believe that they will avail for the conception and the easy delivery of children. A peculiar feature of the festival is that the Luperci also sacrifice a dog."[2]

In this passage it is significant that Plutarch does not name the god in whose honor the Lupercalia was celebrated. The Romans, in fact, associated many deities with the Lupercalia: Lupercus, Faunus, Inuus, Februus, and, more frequently than any Roman god, Pan, or Pan Lycaeus.[3] They seem, furthermore, to have connected the festival with Juno, since the strips with which the Luperci smote the women were called *ami cula Iunonis*.[4] Thus the Romans seem to have had no definite idea of the patron god of the Lupercalia. To decide, if possible, what god was originally worshipped at the wolf's cave will be an important point in our study.

Though they knew so little of the deity of the Lupercalia, the Romans had definite ideas about its purpose. Very frequently the blows dealt by the Luperci are mentioned as assuring to women productivity. In later times this idea of propagation was extended also to the crops.[5] In the minds of the ancients fertility was closely related to purification, for it was by purification from evil powers that the forces of life became active.[6] Consequently by the time of Varro the Lupercalia was regarded as one of the most important lustrations of the state.[7] The idea that the Lupercalia would keep away misfortune of all sorts, such as pestilence, barrenness, famine, war, drought, hail, and tempest, was stressed during later years. Again and again Pope Gelasius chided the people for attributing all these disasters to the cessation of the Lupercalia.[8] These interpretations of the Greeks and the Romans are essentially consistent, being merely different versions of the same idea, for the apotropaic rite which serves to banish evil or to render it inactive results in the freeing of all beneficent forces.

The Lupercalia was probably founded even before the Romans settled on the Palatine,[9] and it continued until 495 A.O., when it was abolished by the edict of Pope Gelasi us.[10] This long existence gives the natural explanation both of the incongruous ritual acts which composed the ceremonial, and of the ignorance of the Romans concerning the presiding deity. The Lupercalia should be studied, not as the product of a particular period, but as a cult complex.[11] It was, in a measure, an epitome of the religious experience of the Romans, and, like a vital organism, it developed now one side, now another, according to the needs of a people that passed from the state of simple shepherds to that of the masters of the world.

NOTES
1. Plut., *Rom.*, 21. 31.
2. In addition to the above cult-features, there were offered at the Lupercalia the *mola salsa*, or salt cakes, which were made by the Vestal Virgins from the first grain of the harvest. These cakes were also offered at the Vestalia and on the Ides of September (Serv. ad Verg., *Eel.*, 8. 82). This is obviously a ceremony that is associated primarily with the ritual of the Vestal Virgins rather than with the Lupercalia, and an adequate explanation of it would involve a survey of the cult of Vesta. Hence it cannot be

included in the present study.

Ovid *(Fast.,* 2. 282) says that the Flamen Dialis officiated at the Lupercalia; but Dr. Fowler *(R. F.,* 313) points out the impossibility of his having performed the sacrifice, since it was unlawful for him to touch either a goat or a dog. It is impossible to explain the presence of the Flamen Dialis at the Lupercalia without an examination of the history and the significance of that obscure minister. Hence that too, like the offering of the *mola salsa,* lies outside the scope of the present study.

3. For the discussion of these various deities, see pp. 36-8, 82 n. 55.

4. See p. 62. O.M.

5. Lyd., *de Mens.,* 4.25.

6. Rohde, i, 247; Samter, *Die Familienfesten der Griechen und Romer,*12.

7. Var., *L. L.,* 6. 34.

8. Gelas., *adv. Androm.,* 13, 21, 24, *et al.*

9. See pp. 38-9 O.M.

10. Baronius, *Annal. Eccles.,* viii, 60 fol.

11. This theory is advocated by Dr. Deubner, *Lupercalia,* in *Archiv für Religionswissenschaft,* vol. xiii, 1910, 481, *et passim.*

CHAPTER III

The Wolf-Deity in Greece

IN EXAMINING THE separate details of the Lupercalia, the first question that arises is, "What did the wolf have to do with the festival?" An overwhelming number of scholars feel that the names *Lupercal, Lupercalia,* and *Luperci* are all derived from *lupus.*[1] Moreover, the cave of the Lupercal is too closely associated with Rome's sacred wolf, the foster mother of Romulus and Remus, for that name, at least, to be derived from anything but *lupus.* It was at that cave that the. Luperci offered sacrifice, and from there they started on their course about the city.[2] Assuming, consequently, that the wolf had some part in the Lupercalia, let us consider the role that the wolf played in the religion of early Greece.

We have evidence that the wolf was regarded as a sacred animal among the Pelasgians. Numerous seals of Minoan Crete bear the figure of a wolf,[3] though it had no such important part in Cretan cults as had the snake and the bull. Yet a Mycenaean seal portrays two wolves standing in heraldic fashion on each sioe of a pillar, in a position similar to that of the lions over Mycenae's gate.[4] In view of the sanctity of the pillar in Mycenaean cults, and the frequent representation of it with heraldic animals,[5] the wolves that stand on each side of this pillar must be accepted as sacred. Throughout the Peloponnesus the wolf-god Lycaeus was highly venerated.   The name *Lycaeus* is generally accepted as meaning *wolf*.[6] Sometimes *Lycaeus* is used alone, but more frequently it becomes an epithet attached to the name of one of the more familiar deities, as *Zeus Lycaeus, Pan Lycaeus,* or *Apollo Lycaeus.* In Arcadia, above all other places, the cult of this god was deep-rooted and wide-spread. There, on Mount Lycaeus, the Lycaea was held in his honor every nine years. On this mountain was the city of Lycosura, the oldest, says Pausanias, in all Greece.[7] Both the city and the festival were said to have been founded by Lycaon, the son of Pelasgus.[8] In this mytho-logical fashion the Greeks expressed their belief that the Lycaea was a religious ceremony of the Pelasgians. As the Lycaea was by most ancient authorities regarded as the prototype of the Lupercalia, it must be carefully examined.

The god in whose honor the Lycaea was celebrated was a dread and mysterious creature. His shrine was sacrosanct, and all men were forbidden to enter it. Anyone who disregarded this prohi-bition would surely die, it was believed, within the year. Consequent-ly the precinct of Lycaeus was for animals a place of refuge, since no hunter would pursue them within its limits. The uncanny nature of the shrine is shown by the belief that within it all creatures lost their shadows.[9] Close by the sanctuary there seems to have been a pool and an oak tree, where, in times of drought, the priest of Zeus Lycaeus was wont to take a branch of the oak tree, stir the water with it, and thus secure the desired rain.[10]

Lycaeus was for men a destructive power to be shunned; but he was the protector of animals. He was also the sender of the rain. Since no shadow was cast within his sanctuary, his realm seems to have been beneath the earth, where the sun's rays might not penetrate.[11] In all these elements we see the characte ristic features of the earth-god.

The Lycaea had the savage rites of many chthonic festivals. Pausanias tells us that even in his day a child was sacrificed, his blood sprinklea upon the altar, and his entrails tasted sacramentally by the priest. Thereupon, say the legends, he who had tasted of the entrails was transformed into a werwolf for the period of nine years.[12] One account tells of a certain Demaenetus who, having partaken of the sacrifice and been changed into a wolf, swam across a pool (probably the one near the shrine of Lycaeus), and entered upon his nine-year exile. At the end of that time he was restored to human form and returned to MountLycaeus.[13]

The sacrifice at the Lycaea was evidently of the expiatory type, the child being offered to appease the savage wolf-god and to divert his malignant power from the people. This is an especially common type of human sacrifice, and of frequent occurrence in the cults of chthonic deities.[14] In ceremonies of this sort, the whole or a part of the victim is sometimes eaten, the idea being that, having been offered to the god, it partakes of his divinity; and so the priest, upon eating the victim, secures this magic power for himself.[15] Yet, because the sacrifice is, in a measure, identified with the god, it becomes a sin to slay it and to eat of its flesh, even though those acts are necessary for the welfare of the people. Consequently the slayer seeks by flight to escape the result of his sacrilege.[16] Often he must undergo some lustral experience.

These ideas appear in other Greek rites. Every ninth year, at Delphi, occurred a ceremony known as the Stepteria, which was supposed to commemorate Apollo's slaughter of the Python and his consequent exile. A hut was built which represented the abode of the Python. A boy, escorted by other boys, set fire to this hut; then they all fled without looking back, and the leader pretended to go into exile. Later they went to Tempe, were purified, and on their way home partook of a feast.[17] Another curious rite, known as the Bouphonia, was performed at Athens. At the sacrifice of an ox, one man felled the ox with an axe and immediately fled. Another man cut the throat of the ox with a knife and, it seems, also fled.Later a formal trial was held to discover who was guilty of the murder of the ox. Each of the participants in the sacrifice blamed someone else, until, finally, the axe and the knife were pronounced guilty and thrown into the sea.[18] Likewise, at Tenedos a new born calf, having been treated as a baby, was sacrificed; the man who killed it was pelted with stones, and finally fled into the sea.[19] Though these rites differ in detail, they have the same basic idea as the Lycaea: a holy victim has been slain, and the slayer flees from the scene of his crime and undergoes some form of penalty.

In the Lycaea this idea has become mingled with another, as so often happens in early rites. The worshipper by partaking of the fare of the wolf Lycaeus is to some extent assimilated to the nature of the god,[20] that is, he becomes "wolfish". In time this idea passed naturally enough into the belief that he became a werwolf. Furthermore, it has been suggested that the priests honored their deity by disguising themselves as wolves.[21] This would have been in accord with the numerous animal disguises pictured on Cretan seals.[22] Such a practice would aid in the development of the werwolf legend.

Lycaon changes in a wolf, Hendrick Goltzius, 1589

The deity of the Lycaea is usually given as *Zeus Lycaeus,* but Varro and Isidorus name him *"Lycaeus,* the especial god of the Arcadians." [23] This recognition of Lycaeus as the original deity of the festival is certainly right. The ceremony is far removed from the seemly homage paid to the Olympian Zeus. The Lycaean Zeus is a composite of the Hellenic sky-god superimposed upon the wolf-shaped spirit of Mount Lycaeus.[24] Zeus, as usual, usurped the place of honor, and the name of Lycaeus was reduced to a mere appellative. But in all except the name Lycaeus remained unchanged; he was still the wolf-god, demanding his tribute of human flesh. Of the struggle that ensued between the rival cults of Zeus and of Lycaeus, legend gives us a clear picture: the sons of Lycaon, desiring to propitiate Zeus, sacrificed to him a child and served the entrails to his priest; but Zeus in wrath destroyed by lightning Lycaon and all his sons except the youngest.[25] This myth expresses the horror which the Hellenes had for a barbarous rite. They strove to abolish it, but the lightnings of Zeus had only temporary power. Ultimately the older cult prevailed, and Zeus accepted the strange sacrifice offered to him.

Pan, another Arcadian god, also became associated with Lycaeus. This seems to have been nothing more than the natural union of two deities worshipped in the same locality, for Pan too, had his shrine and sacred grove on Mont Lycaeus.[26] By later writers, especially among the Romans, Zeus Lycaeus was almost wholly displaced by Pan Lycaeus. This was not strange. The wolfgod was in time obscured, and his name became merely an adjectiv. Ancient scholars, when trying to explain that name, interpreted it as "he who keeps the wolves from the herds"[27] This title was meaningless when applied to Zeus, but expressed a very natural part of Pan's functions. Thus in time, though thoughtful students like Varro, Pliny, or Pausanias knew that the Lycaea was in honor of Lycaeus or Zeus Lycaeus, less critical ones attributed it to Pan Lycaeus. In view of the fact that writers of the Empire regarded Pan Lycaeus as the god of the Lupercalia, it is important to understand him as merely the poetic equivalent of Zeus Lycaeus. In other parts of Hellas, Lycaeus was absorbed by Apollo.The Pelasgian city of Argos [28] venerated its shrine of Apollo Lycaeus as the most ancient and most noteworthy of all,[29] and stamped its coins with the image of Apollo Lycaeus.[30] There, we are told, a wolf was sacrificed to Apollo "the wolfslayer".[31] Porphyrius seems to indicate that at times a wolf was eaten sacramentally; for he cites various animals sacred to different deities, among them, the wolf to Apollo Lycaeus. Then he goes on: "And when persons sacrifice and eat these animals, they give a foolish reason".[32] Very rarely do we hear of a wild animal being sacrificed in Greece.[33] It is often interpreted as a relic of totemism, the animal embodiment of the god being sacrificed as the god's most acceptable victim, and being eaten sacramentally by the worshippers.[34]

In Athens traces of the wolf's sacred character remained in the law that anyone who killed a wolf must erect at his own expense a tomb in its honor.[35] There was also a cult of Apollo Lycaeus and a priest devoted to his service.[36] His abode was the cave at the foot of the Acropolis; and it continued in the historical period to be sacred to Apollo.[37] In time the sacred wolf seems to have been reduced to a local hero, Lycus, whose statue was of wolf-form.[38] It is easy to trace in this material the development of religious belief. First, the deity was pure wolf, Lycaeus; then, grafted upon the Olympian god, he became Apollo Lycaeus; ultimately legend explained the honor shown to the wolf by creating a hero, Lycus.

At Delphi one of the months was named Lycaeus;[39] and close by Apollo's altar stood a great bronze statue of a wolf, which was said to have saved the temple treasures from a thief.[40] The wolf was not a strange figure at an oracle; in other places, too, it was believed to have oracular power.[41]

In Asia Minor and on the Aegean islands we find survivals of Apollo, the wolf-god. Lycia, whose name is believed to have been derived from *Lycaeus*,[42] was the center of the worship, and there Apollo kept his primitive wolf-form.[43] Later he was regarded as the god who drove away the wolves, and his shrine in Lycia gained great fame on this account.[44] In Tarsus coins similar to the Mycenaean seal mentioned above [45] portrayed Apollo standing between two wolves and holding their paws in his hands.[46] Latona, when fleeing from Juno, was guided by wolves to Lycia, or to Delos, and to escape detection, she herself assumed the form ot a wolf.[47] In Crete Apollo on various occasions disguised himself as a wolf.[48] There he employed wolves to protect and feed his infant son Miletus, who had been exposed in the woods.[49] This story offers a close parallel to the tale of the wolf-nurse of Romulus and Remus.

In the majority of cases Lycaeus, when absorbed by one of the higher gods, became kindly and gracious. A legend of Temesa in Southern Italy shows him in his true character. A drunken sailor of Ulysses, the story runs, had ravished a maiden of Temesa, and was in punishment stoned to death by the people. He became a vengeful ghost, preying upon the inhabitants of that place. They appealed to the Pythian oracle, and were directed to appease the creature by giving him every year the fairest maiden of Temesa for his wife. But one year the maiden to be sacrificed had a lover who fought with the ghost, and drove him into the sea. In an old painting this ghost, named Lycas, is portrayed as black and wearing a wolf-skin.[50] In this tale the wolf-god is frankly a creature of the underworld, who devours men as his prey.

She-wolf suckling Romulus en Remus, Giovanni Battista Galestruzzi, 1625 - 1669

The same conception appears in a legend of Apollo Lycaeus which is told by Phlegon.[51] A Roman commander at Naupactus prophesied that he would be devoured by a red wolf, and bade his followers offer the beast no resistance. The wolf came and devoured the Roman, leaving only his head. When the people approached to bury it, the head forbade them to touch it, saying that Apollo through the wolf, his minister, had led the dead man to the seats of the blessed. Thereupon the people erected a shrine to Apollo Lycaeus. Though this tale is late, Dr. Reinach believes that it reflects very ancient beliefs. The wolf, he says, typifies death; he was a power that none might withstand, hence the command of the Roman to his soldiers that they witness his death in passive acquiescence.[52] It is in accord with this interpretation that Hades appeared at times clad in a wolf-skin,[53] which indicates that he was once thought of as wolf-shaped.[54]

The cult of the wolf-god in Greece had its oldest centers in regions whose Pelasgian stock mingled but slightly with the Aryans, that is, Arcadia and Lycia. In other places that held tenaciously to their earth-cults, as Argos, Attica, and Delphi, the wolf-god remained, though he was often modified or absorbed by an Olympian god. Sometimes he was reduced to the wolf-formed spirit that kept the wolves from the fold. But in more primitive times the wolf, prowling in darkness and preying upon men and cattle, was an embodiment of the destructive power of the earth. His worship, therefore, arose largely from fear; and sacrifices Were offered to him in order to appease him, that he might not slay the people. Thus he was a characteristic earth-god of the Pelasgians.

NOTES

1. See pp. 36-7, 45 n. 63, 64; 46 n. 69 O.M..

2. Var., *L. L.*, 5. 85; Serv. ad Verg.. *Aen.*, 8. 343.

3. Evans, *Ser. Min.*, 209.

4. Farnell, iv, 116 n. 6;

5. Evans, *J. H. S.*, vol. xxi, l53-63.

6. Farnell, iv, 113; Wernicke, in Pauly-Wissowa, ii, 59.7.

7. Paus., 8. *2*. l; 8. 38. r.

8. Paus., 8. *2*. r.

9. Paus., 8. 38. 6; Polyb., r6 . 12. 7; Schol. ad Callim., *Hym. in lcr11.*, 13. 10. Paus., 8. 38. 4; Aug., *de Civ. Dei*, 18. 17.

11. Immerwahr, *Die Kulte und Mythen Arkadiens*, 18; Fick, 132.

12. Paus., 8. 2. 3, 6; 8. 37. 8: Plat., *de Rep.*, 565d; id. *Minos*, 315; Theophr. ap. Porphyr., *de Abst.*, 2. 27.

13. Plin., *N. H.*, 8. 82; Aug., *de Civ. Dei*, 18. 17.

14. These statements are based upon the analysis of human sacrifice made by Dr. Westermarck, i, 65-70, 437-72.

15. Westermarck, i, 63, ii, 562-4.

16. Farnell, iii, 93; Harrison, lll n. 1,112-14.

17. Plut. *de Defect. Orac.*, 14; Ael. *Var. Hist.*, 3. l. See also Harrison,113-14.

18. Porphyr. *de Abst.*, 2. 29 fol.; Ael., *Var. Hist.*, 8. 3. See also Smith, *The Religion of the Semites*, 304-6; Harrison, lll.

19. Ael., *N. A.*, 12. 34.

20. Nilsson, *Griechische Feste*, 10.

21. Frazer, *The Golden Bough*, iv, 83; Reinach, *Cultes*, ii,211.

22. See p.6. O.M.

23. Var. ap. Aug., *de Civ. Dei*, 18. 17; lsid. *Orig.*, 8. 9. 5.

24. Klausen, *Aeneas und die Penaten*, ii, 1232. For a full survey of Zeus Lycaeus, see A. B. Cook, *Zeus*, 63--99; Immerwahr, 1-24.

25. Apollod., *Bibl.*, 3. 8. r.

26. For the character and history of Pan, see chapter V.

27. Serv. ad Verg., *Aen.*, 8.343.

28. Smith, *Dictionary of Geography*, i,202.

29. Paus., 2. 19. 3; Schol. ad Soph., *Elec.*,6.

30. *C. I. G.*, i. rug. *2*.

31. Schol. ad Soph., *Elec.*,6.

32. Porphyr., *de Abst.*, 3. l7.

33. At Brauron a bear was sacrificed to Artemis (Schol. ad Aristoph., *Lysi st.*,645). At Patrae in honor of Artemis Laphria wild animals of many kinds were cast alive upon the altar fire (Paus.,7.18.12).

34. This is the view of Dr. Frazer, (viii, 310-12) and of Dr. Farnell (i, 41). The limited compass of the present study makes it necessary to omit any consideration of the vexed question of totemism, inasmuch as it was possible for the wolf to be

worshipped as a god without its being a totem animal (Farnell, in *Year's Work in Classical Studies,* rgo8, 71).

35. Schol. ad Ap. Rhod., *2*. 124.

36. *Ath. Mitth.,* 1901, 213 ; *C. I. A.,* iii. 1. 292.

37. Eur., *Ion,*10.

38. Paus., I. 19. 3; Aristoph., *Vesp.,* 389. 39.

39. *Bull. Hell.,* v, 1881, 429. 5, Inscr.43.

40. Paus., JO. 14. 7; Plut., *Pericl.,* 21; Ael., *H . A.,* JO. 26.

41. Farnell, iv, 117; Furtwängler, in Roscher, i,443.

42. Farnell, iv,112.

43. Bode, *Scriptores rerum mythicarum,* Cellis 1834, iii, 16, page209.

44. Paul. ex. Fest., I19.

45. See p. 2I O.M.

46. Farnell, iv,309.

47. Ael., *H. A.,* JO. 26; Aristot., *Hist. Anim.,* 6. 35; Ap. Rhod., 2. 124; Anton. Liber., 35.

48. Serv. ad Verg., *Aen.,* 4.377.

49. Anton. Liber.,30.

50. Paus:, 6. 6. 7-11; Strab., 6. I . 5.

51. *Mirab.* eh.3.

52. Reinach, *Cultes,* i, 296 n.4.

53. In the tomb-paintings of Etruria, Hades wears a wolf-skin helmet (Cook, *Zeus,* Fig. 72, 73).

54. Reinach, *Cultes,* i, 295.

CHAPTER IV

The Wolf-Deity in Italy

THE WOLF-CULTS of Italy present the appearance of a religious survival from a remote time. Of an actual wolf-god, we find far fewer manifestations than in Greece. Yet in the realm of magic, augury, and popular superstition, the wolf was more conspicuous and more highly venerated in Italy than was any other anima.[1] Since an outgrown religion regularly lingers, often through many centuries, as a superstition or a magic 'practice, the widespread belief in the uncanny power of wolves indicates that at some time the wolf was important in Italian religion. The actual cults connected with the wolf are those of the obscure deity Soranus, of Mars, and of the little-known Lupercusor Luperca, who was named by some ancient scholars as the deity of the Lupercalia.[2] In studying these wolf-cults, we shall seek to learn whether they originated among the Ligurians or the Aryans of Italy, and whether the ceremonial acts were similar to those performed in Greece in honor of the chthonic wolf, or akin to the rites of Olympian gods. That will give us a basis to interpret the ritual of the Lupercalia.

Near Rome, in the country of the Faliscans, was a wolf-cult

that was associated with Soranus, the god of Mount Soracte. The ritual combined the features of a fire-cult and a wolf-cult. Every year the priests performed a rite in which they walked through blazing coals, and yet were not burned.[3] Fire-cults were rare in the religion of either the Greeks or the Romans. This particular one seems the natural product of the location, for the land of the Faliscans was volcanic, with numerous chasms whence issued pestiferous fumes.[4] In this region, consequently, fire was the prime manifestation of the earth-spirit. Hephaistus, too, the product of like forces, was a chthonic god, embodying the subterranean fire.[5] The wolf-element of the cult appears in the name of the priests, *Hirpi Sorani, hirpi* being the Sabine name for *wolves.* It appears also in the following legend.[6] At one time when the Hirpi were sacrificing, wolves suddenly appeared and snatched from the fire the entrails of the sacrifice. Shepherds pursued the wolves to a cave, from which were emitted such deadly fumes that those standing near were killed. A pestilence followed because the wolves had been molested. This could be allayed, the Hirpi learned from an oracle, if they would *imitate the wolves.* This imitation of the wolves Servius interpreted as *rapto vivere.*[6] But aetiological myths like this one, regularly try to explain the details of the ceremony. Thus the story indicates that the Hirpi, in imitation of wolves, put on wolf-skins as a ceremonial garb,[7] devoured the entrails of the victim, and then took to flight with the people in pursuit. The rite shows, therefore, strong similarity to the Lycaea[8] in each festival the priests, perhaps clad in wolf-skins, partook ceremonially of the sacrificial victim, and then fled to escape pollution for their sacrilege; each band of priests underwent an expiatory experience, in the one case through exile, in the other through flight and through breathing the fumes from the cavern.

The spirit of Mount Soracte was perhaps wolf-shaped, and manifested himself in volcanic fire and pestilential vapors. His power expressed, not the beneficent, but the destructive, activity of the earth: he was a death-god.[9] His name, meaning "the god of Soracte," was derived from the mountain that he inhabited, and was in later times felt to be nothing more than a vague description. Some ancient scholars, therefore, identified him with Apollo,[10] to whom also the wolf was sacred. Servius, understanding the true nature of Soranus, said that he was also called Dis, since Mount Soracte was consecrated to the *Di Manes*.[11]

The Hirpi Sorani were a very small group of families living about Mount Soracte.[12] Such veneration attached to their sacred function that they were freed by decree of the senate from all military or other service.[12] The view of some authorities, that the Hirpi were Sabines,[13] seems to me most improbable. Mount Soracte was located in the land of the Faliscans; and the cult was obviously a product of the mountain, wolf-infested, and expressing the deadly power of the underworld by volcanic fire and by noxious exhalations. Such a cult surely could not have been imported. Nor is it reasonable to suppose that the Sabines, some of whom settled among the Faliscans,[14] developed the cult after their arrival. The worship of Soranus has all the marks of hoar antiquity; it is intensely local, and appears in no other region of Italy. Contrasted with these reasons against supposing that Soranus was a Sabine god, we have on the positive side only the fact that *hirpus* was the Sabine name for wolf.[15]

Wolf, Jacobus Cornelis Gaal, after Johann Elias Ridinger, 1850

No one states that Sabines were the worshippers.[16] That a Sabine name should have become attached to the priests of Soranus is wholly natural. Just as the Sabines introduced many of their words into the Latin language, so the Sabine settlers near Falerii may well have given their own name to the priests of Soranus.

It is likewise improbable that the Hirpi Sorani were Faliscans. The statement that they were a very few families living in the land of the Faliscans [12] certainly indicates that they were a separate group. Their meager numbers are strongly suggestive of an earlier people, who, in the fastness of their mountain, kept their individuality and their peculiar religion. Archaeology proves that the neighborhood of Falerii was occupied during the Neolithic Age.[17] It also supports the assumption that these neolithic folk, or Ligurians, continued in their old home after the coming of the Aryans, for both cremation-urns and inhumation-graves have been found about Falerii; and they seem to be contemporaneous.[18] Legends of Falerii tell that it was occupied successively by Siculi, by Argives, by Faliscans, who were closely related to the Romans, and by Sabines.[19] Dionysius commented upon the traces of Pelasgian origin that persisted in Falerii in his own day.[20]

Therefore we may conclude that the god of Mount Soracte was a chthotiic deity of the Mediterranean people. He was similar to Zeus Lycaeus, being embodied in a wolf, and being a merciless god of destruction.

Another wolf-cult of Falerii is of more immediate interest in our study of the Lupercalia, for the goddess, or priestess, of the cult was named Valeria Luperca. We hear of it through only one writer, though it continued until a late date. At one time, the legend runs,[21] a fearful pestilence fell upon the Faliscans. An oracle told them that the plague would be stayed if they should sacrifice every year a maiden to Juno; accordingly a girl named Valeria Luperca was chosen as the victim. But when the sword was drawn, an eagle, swooping down, seized it and thrust it into a cow that was grazing near; then placed upon the altar a small hammer. This was taken up, by the maiden, who went to each of the sick, touched him with it, and bade him be healed.

This story suggests the legend of Iphigenia, in its main situation of a maiden who, when about to be sacrificed, was saved by the substitution of an animal victim. Iphigenia is usually interpreted as a cult-title of Artemis, or as an early goddess who was later identified with Artemis.[22] The story of her escape from death seems a recollection of the time when human sacrifice was abolished and an animal substituted. The same explanation is a natural one for the story of Valeria Luperca. Just as Iphigenia was later replaced by Artemis and reduced to a priestess, so Valeria Luperca was subordinated to Juno. Nowhere else do we hear of a human victim being offered to Juno; therefore we can hardly believe that she was the original deity honored in this ceremony. The goddess Luperca, however, whose name is most reasonably derived from *lupa*, a wolf,[23] would, like the wolf-gods of Greece, very naturally have been honored by a human sacrifice. The rite evidently antedated the coming of the *terramara* folk, for the maiden was saved by an eagle, the bird of the Romans. The legend indicates, therefore, a barbarous rite that was ·ended by the northern immigrants.

The importance of the hammer in the legend leads us, as does the name of the priestess, to the Valerii, a gens who lived near the Faliscans, for they adopted *Acisculus* as a cognomen, and employed the emblem of the hammer on many of their coins.[24] This sacred hammer reminds us of the weapon-cult which was prominent in the religion of Minoan Crete,[25] thus strengthening the view that Valeria

Luperca was a goddess of the Ligurians.

We may reconstruct the legend as follows. Luperca was a local goddess of the Ligurians living near Falerii. The Valerian gens took over her cult, but abolished the practice of human sacrifice. Henceforth the goddess was known as Valeria Luperca.[26] In time this local deity was absorbed by Juno; and only an obscure legend and the sacred hammer which was the emblem of the Valerii showed that she had everexisted.

That the wolf was known throughout Italy as the sacred animal of Mars is a literary commonplace that needs no amplification here. Since the name of Mars, which comes from the Iudo-European root *mar-*, meaning *brightness*,[27] appears in many of the Italic dialects, and since the worship of Mars was important in all the lands occupied by the Aryan invaders,[28] Mars is generally accepted as the chief god whom the *terramara* folk brought with them into Italy.[29] Yet there is much in the ancient cults and the character of Mars that is like the Mediterranean nature-spirits rather than the Aryan gods. The importance of Mars in lustral and agrarian rites, especially those of the spring, and his association with the ancient Dea Dia, leads Roscher, who has made the most exhaustive examination of the cults of Mars,[30] to conclude that Mars was a god of spring and summer who was closely connected with the crops, the cattle, health, and sickness. Dr. Fowler, who accepts the conclusions of Roscher, says of the month that was named for Mars: "Some great *numen* is at work, quickening vegetation, and calling into life the powers of reproduction in man and the animals. ...It was this Power, we can hardly doubt, that the Latins knew by the name of Mars, the god whose cult is so prominent throughout the critical period of the quickening processes."[31] Such a god corresponds in all respects to the earth-god of the Mediterranean race.

As a result, we must believe that the Mars of historical times was a composite deity, the Aryan god having absorbed much of the nature and the ritual of the Mediterranean deities who were already in possession of the land. This fusion is shown in the case of two local deities of Liguria who are called respectively Cemenelus or Mars Cemenelus,[32] and Mars Leucimalacus.[33] In like manner it is reasonable to believe, though impossible to prove, that Mars absorbed a wolf-deity of the Ligurians, and that the wolf was in time reduced to his attendant animal. In association with Mars, the wolf lost much of his savage character, and became a helpful animal that guided colonists on their way,[34] and rescued Romulus and Remus, the infant sons of Mars.[35] Just so, when associated with Apollo, did Lycaeus grow gentle.

We come now to the main point of this investigation, the part of the wolf in the Lupercalia. Was there in the neighborhood of Rome before the arrival of the *terramara* invaders a Ligurian populace who might have been the authors of a wolf-cult? Archaeology, unfortunately, gives us only meager help in this problem. The hills of Rome have been densely populated for so long a time that it is very difficult to find any remains that unquestionably date back even to the regal period.[36] We do know, however, that the immediate neighborhood was inhabited from remote times; for in the gravels of the Tiber and the Anio have been found flints belonging to the Palaeolithic Age.[37] Even as close to Rome as the Mulvian Bridge was found a rich collection of very early stone implements, together with bones of extinct animals.[38] But in the types of tombs found in Rome itself we have the clearest evidence. In the ancient cemeteries on the Esquiline and in the Forum, inhumation was the more common form of burial, and the skulls found in these graves were dominantly dolichocephalic.[39]

Many traditions tell that before the arrival of the Romans there were persons living upon the site of Rome.[40] These settlers are known as Ligurians, Siculi, or Pelasgians; Dionysius designates them as autochthonous, and says that not a few traces of them continued there even in his time.[41] Testifying to the truth of these traditions are various ancient shrines. On the lower slope of the Cermalus there was, close by the Lupercal, the sacred fig-tree, an emblem of Rumina, goddess of fecundity;[42] and, at the foot of the hill in the Velabrum, the shrine, or tomb, of Acea Larentia, which was the seat of an ancient grave-cult.[43] On the Aventine were places sacred to Bona Dea, Faunus, Picus, and Evander; and, at the foot of the hill, the shrines of Murcia, Heracles, and Consus.[44] Cacus was localized both on the Aventine and on the Palatine.[45] On the Capitoline were the grave of Tarpeia,[46] the altar to Saturnus,[47] and, near the foot, the shrine to Carmenta.[48] All these deities and their cults were distinctly chthonic. The gods presided over fertility, prophecy, or death, and all, according to the legends, antedated the founding of Rome.

From this evidence of archaeology, of legend, and of cult, we are justified in believing that when the Romans settled on the Palatine they found the Ligurians already established in the neighborhood, and that they adopted from these Ligurians many of the cults that were inseparably attached to places later included within the Roman city.[49]

One of the prominent natural objects of the Palatine was the Lupercal, a large cavern, with a spring issuing from it, with the sacred *Ficus Ruminalis* closeby, and with dense woods all about.[50] Since a site like that was, in the eyes of a primitive people, a particularly natural place for the abode of a deity, the probabilities are all in favor of a cult having been established at the Lupercal by the oldest settlers in the region.[51] Moreover, the veneration shown to the *Ficus Ruminalis* is evidently, Dr. Evans believes, of Mediterranean origin, since the fig-tree was devoutly worshipped throughout the lands near the Mediterranean, but was almost unknown in Central Europe.[52]

Associated with this cave was the well-known tale of the wolf who was foster-mother to Romulus and Remus. It is significant that in the oldest versions of that tale the wolf was the all-important actor. Dionysius tells how the wolf cared for the babes, and then, upon the arrival of the shepherds, retired to the Lupercal with such deliberation and dignity that the shepherds believed her to be under the guidance of some god.[53] In this version the human beings had a secondary part in the preservation of the twins; Faustulus was not present at the rescue, and his wife was nameless and insignificant. Dionysius supports his tale with a long list of authorities: Fabius Pictor, Cincius Alimentus, Cato, Calpurnius Piso, and numerous others. This version, that the rescue was due to a real wolf, constantly appears in history and in epic.[54]

Since the wolf acted under Mars's direction for the rescue of his sons, she belongs with the wolves of Apollo who cared for his son.[55] The Roman story, like the Greek one, suggests an animal god who was later replaced by a human one. We may believe, then, that the wolf of the Lupercal, originally honored as a deity, passed through the same development as did Lycaeus, and was reduced to the sacred animal of Mars. But the wolf could not be wholly banished from her ancient seat. Therefore, when story tellers portrayed the origin of Rome, they accounted for the homage which the Romans gave to the wolf-deity by making her the foster-mother of Rome's founder.[56]

Helmeted head of Roma, She-wolf standing, suckling the twins (Remus and Romulus); shepherd Faustulus standing; in background, birds on fig tree

Later rationalists sought to remove the wolf from the story through the explanation that *lupa,* which was the common designation of a *meretrix,* was a term that had been applied to the wife of Faustulus.[57] To provide her with a name, they identified her with Acea Larentia, an ancient goddess whose shrine was near the Lupercal.[58] This identification was not necessarily an arbitrary assumption, based upon the proximity of two shrines. Acea Larentia was, as has been shown by Professor Pais, a form of the earth-deity, who was known to the Romans by a variety of names: Tellus, Terra, Ops, Maia, Bona Dea, Fauna, Fatua, Dea Dia, and Ceres.[59] Thus she was closely akin to the chthonic wolf. Professor Pais even goes so far as to suggest that she was originally honored as a real wolf.[60]

Our next question is whether this wolf-deity, venerated throughout Italy, enshrined in the Lupercal, and prominent in Rome's early legends, was the god in whose honor the Lupercalia was celebrated. That festival was associated with various deities. Can any one of them be interpreted as the wolf-god? In answer to this question, one naturally thinks of Lupercus, who was occasionally named as the god of the festival.[61]

The exact meaning of the name *Lupercus* has been since the days of Roman scholarship a matter of dispute. Servius suggests a variety of interpretations.[62] The one most generally accepted by modern authorities is that *Lupercus* came from *lupus+arceo,* and so meant "he who keeps off the wolves;"[63] that is, the Luperci were "the wolf-averters." To this idea the weighty objection has been raised that a wolf-averting festival was strangely localized at the lair of the beneficent wolf who rescued Rome's founder, and that it offered, moreover, no explanation of the abiding hold which the Lupercalia had upon the urban populace of Rome.[64] Another explanation offered by Servius, and supported by Ovid,[65] is that the Lupercal was named in honor of the wolf which rescued Romulus and Remus. In agreement with this view is the statement of Lactantius, that Lupa, the nurse of Romulus, was accorded divine honors.[66] Varro, a more valuable authority, actually identified the wolf with the goddess Luperca. [67] "The savage wolf", he says, "for her kindness to the babes, was named the goddess Luperca." It is noteworthy that Varro uses the feminine form of the name: that is added proof of its antiquity, for in many cases the female deity was the primitive one, but was later displaced by her male double. Varro's statement seems to controvert the view which has been advanced,[68] that Lupercus was merely a late abstraction manufactured from the festival. We seem justified, therefore, in believing that there was a wolf-formed spirit of the Lupercal, who was known as *Lupa, Lu perca,* or *Lupercus.*[69]

As a matter of fact, the two explanations of the name Lupercus which are offered by Servius seem to reflect two different stages in the history of the god. These two stages appear very clearly in the names of the wolf-god of Greece. In Arcadia he was called *Lycaeus,* "the wolf-like"; in Argos, where he was identified with Apollo, the compound name was *Apollo Lycaeus.* But the wolf-god was later explained as "he who destroys the wolves", therefore Apollo's appellation became Λυκοκτόνος "the wolf-slayer."[70] In like manner, the Delphian Apollo was called both Πύθιος [71] and Πυθοκτόνος [72] Dr. Graillot explains this by saying that Apollo was first identified with the chthonic serpent, and later regarded as its slayer.[73] Similarly, Artemis was called both Ἐλαφεία [74] and Ἐλαφηβόλος.[75] This is a development that constantly appears in ancient religion, for when a primitive animal-deity had faded into the mere epithet of an anthropomorphic god, scholars, at a loss to account for the significance of the animal in the cult, explained it, in case the animal was dangerous, by making the god its special foe or, if the animal was useful, its protector. As this explanation entirely disregarded the superstitious veneration that regularly attached to the animal, modern scholars usually rate it no more highly than most of the etymological attempts of the ancients.[76] In like manner, the deity of the Lupercal was probably known in the earliest times as *Lupa* or *Lupus*. Later, when the animal-god had lost prestige, the usual explanation was employed, that the god was a *wolf-averter;* and the name was altered to *Luperca* or *Lupercus*. This explanation obviates all the difficulties arising from the name: it is in harmony with the reverence shown to the wolf-god and to his festival; it adopts an etymology that seems unassailable *(lupus+arceo);* and it is in accord with the development seen in many other cults, in which the homage first given to the animal-god was later given to the deity who destroyed that animal. The name of the god was then extended to his priests, and they were known as Luperci. Mediterranean worshippers often sought in this way to identify themselves with their deity.[77] Thus the devotees of Bacchus called themselves Bacchae, and those of Sabazios or Sabos, Sabazioi or Saboi.[78]

If we grant the existence of the wolf-deity Luperca, it seems inevitable that the Lupercalia, which was celebrated at her cave, was held in her honor. But the Romans also associated the festival with Pan, Pan Lycaeus, Faunus, and Inuus. Justin gives us the clue to this variety of names. He states that there was at the foot of the Palatine a shrine to Lycaeus, whom the Greeks call *Pan,* the Romans *Lupercus*.[79] In other words, Lupercus was regarded as merely the Roman double of Lycaeus. Naturally enough then, Lupercus was also identified with Pan Lycaeus, who had largely displaced Lycaeus in

Arcadia.[80] Consequently the god of the Lupercalia came to be spoken of most frequently as *Pan Lycaeus,* or, the wolf-god being crowded out entirely, as simply *Pan.*[81]

Ovid, who alone names Faunus as the god of the festival, shows clearly that he uses that name as the Roman equivalent of *Pan.* He begins by calling the Lupercalia the festival of *Faunus;* then, to explain its origin, says that because *Pan* was especially honored by the ancient Arcadians, his woodland rites were established in Rome by Evander.[82] Thus Ovid, following the convention of his day, used the names *Faunus* and *Pan* interchangeably. But he then went one step further and identified *Faunus* and *Pan Lycaeus,* asking: "Who denies that the Luperci have their name from the mountain of Arcadia? In Arcadia the Lycaean Faunus has a temple."[83] This is an easy extension for a poet to make: Faunus, being identical with Pan, is also identical with Pan Lycaeus, and consequently, with Lycaeus, the god whom Pan had displaced. Thus Ovid really accepted the general view that Pan Lycaeus was god of the Lupercalia; but he translated Pan Lycaeus into a still more familiar name, Faunus.[84]

The explanation of Inuus as the patron deity of the Lupercalia is still easier to establish. Livy, the only one who associates Inuus with that festival, says that the rite was celebrated in honor of *Pan Lycaeus,* whom the Romans later called *Inuus.*[85]

Probus sums up the whole thing by stating that certain persons regard Pan, Inuus, and Faunus as the same.[86] When, therefore, the Romans spoke of the deity of the Lupercalia as Lupercus, Lycaean Pan, Pan, Faunus, or Inuus, they were merely applying one or

Pan with flute, Jan de Bisschop, 1669

another name to the same god, Lupercus, the Ligurian brother of the Pelasgian Lycaeus.

The cult of Lupercus was wholly different from the usual religious ceremonies of the Romans. It was in type Pelasgian, and Ovid named it Pelasgian.[87] Because of the non-Roman character of the ritual and the similarity of Lupercus to Lycaeus, the majority of the legends about the Lupercalia said that it was founded by the Arcadian exile Evander.[88] The ancients frequently derived the Ligurian populace in various parts of Italy from the Pelasgians, often naming Arcadia as the original home of these settlers,[89] since in historical times Arcadia was the most markedly Pelasgian of any country of Greece.[90] The general belief of the oldest writers that the Lupercalia existed before Rome was founded,[91] shows that they recognized it as the cult of a pre-Roman people. Consequently the germ of truth to be extracted from the legend of the Arcadian origin of the Lupercalia is that it was a festival established by the Ligurians who lived about the site of Rome before the appearance of the Aryans. It had so strong a hold upon the religious imagination, and was so inseparably connected with the Lupercal, that it was taken over by the conquerors. The founders of the festival, however, were so completely absorbed by the *terramara* folk that, when ancient scholars began to speculate about this rite which had all the ear-marks of a Mediterranean cult, they must go outside the bounds of Italy to find its origin.

That the Lupercalia was a festival of the Ligurian race is borne out by the legends of the priests who performed it, the Fabii and the Quintilii.[92] The latter are, in all the accounts, associated with Romulus, and so may be accepted as belonging to the Romans.[93] According to most legends, the Fabii sprang from a daughter of Evander and Hercules.[94] On their mother's side, then, the Fabii were Ligurians. Their father was a non-Roman hero,who arrived at the Palatine before the Romans themselves. Hercules was originally not a god, but a *hero* of the Pelasgians, born at Tiryns and strongly localized in Argolis and in Arcadia.[95] His title Ἀλεξίκακος [96] expressed his power to protect man from evil of every form.[97] This power of universal protection, which is so marked in chthonic deities, is regarded by Dr. Gruppe as the oldest stratum of the Hercules cult, and as the origin of the legends of his twelve labors.[98] Later Hercules was appropriated by theDorians and included among their Olympian deities.[99] But the Hercules to whom Evander dedicated the Ara Maxima,[100] and who became the father of the Fabii, seems to have been the Pelasgian *hero.* He was called *Tirynthius heros,*[101] and was attended by Argives.[102] Thus the Fabii were in their parentage pre-Roman and Pelasgian. The ceremonial acts of the Lupercalia were so numerous and so incoherent that it seems hardly credible that they represent the original form of the festival. They offer, indeed,every appearance of a cult-complex, in which there has been a gradual accretion of ceremonies. In seeking to reconstruct the earliest stage of the Lupercalia, we note that none of the accounts which make the festival antedate the founding of Rome mention the cutting of the goat-skins into thongs, nor the blows dealt by the Luperci to the women. Ovid assigned this ritual act to a later period, and we shall find reason to believe that he was right.[103] Likewise the sacrifice of the dog and the blood-ritual, which were mentioned by Plutarch only, reasonably seem to have been a later development.[104]

Of the ceremonial which was ascribed to the pre-Romans, we have a fairly coherent picture, though authorities vary slightly about the details. At the entrance to the cave, where in later times stood the statue of the She-wolf,[105] a sacrifice was offered. In the earliest days this was presumably a female goat; later, probably when Luperca had been merged into Lupercus, a male goat seems to have been added.[106] After the sacrifice a ritualistic race was performed by the Luperci, who in the earliest times were evidently wholly naked.[107] Most writers place the sacrificial feast after the return of the Luperci from their race,[108] but Ovid, in his lengthy account, says that the Luperci had a slight repast—exigua dapes—before the race, and a feast after it.[109] The natural interpretation is that, immediately after the sacrifice, the Luperci tasted ceremonially of the entrails, as the priest of Lycaeus did after he had sacrificed.[110] Such a rite explains Ovid's words, exigua dapes. Then, at the close of the race, came the feast upon the flesh of the victim.

The descriptions of the Lupercalia assign a different role to the Fabii and to the Quintilii. The two groups of priests evidently did not run together, as the word discursus or an equivalent is regularly used to describe their course.[111] Tubero says that the band of Remus, (i. e. the Fabii,[112]) ran first; and, when they were opposite the Aventine, were attacked by shepherds of Numitor, who threw at them stones, spears, and anything they could lay hands on, and finally captured them; the followers of Romulus did not share in these experiences.[113] They were also evidently debarred from the sacrificial feast, for Ovid tells that in the race they were outstripped by the Fabii, and, upon their arrival at the feast, found the sacrifice entirely consumed, only the bones remaining.[114] It is significant that on that occasion Romulus did not show his usual self-assertion; he merely laughed and regretted that his followers had been outdone by the Fabii. A similar tale is told about the Potitii and the Pinarii, the priests of Hercules: the former arrived first and ate the *exta* of the victim, but the Pinarii reached there only in time to share in the rest of the feast. For this reason the custom continued that the Pinarii should not eat of the entrails.[115] A similar distinction between the Quintilii and the Fabii seems the natural basis of Ovid's story. We may then, believe that, when the Roman priests were admitted to the Ligurian festival, they were debarred from the most significant rites, the flight and the feast. Propertius seems to regard the Fabii as the all-important members of the priesthood, for, in speaking of the Luperci, he mentions the Fabii only. [116]

The fact that the Luperci are invariably spoken of as *running* on their course shows that their speed was an essential feature of the ceremony. This seems to have been overlooked in previous explanations of the festival. Furthermore, they were said to have run naked in order to gain swiftness.[117] The nakedness may, in itself, have been of ritualistic significance;[118] yet certainly, when the Luperci, immediately after the sacrifice and the tasting of the entrails, cast aside their garments and ran forth at top speed, we have every indication of a ritualistic flight. The legends give no evidence that the original race was around the Palatine, as it was in later times.[119] The tale of the pursuit of the cattle-thieves suggests a course away from the village, rather than around it. Plutarch describes this chase by the word ἐκδραμεῖν, while he uses περιτέχειν of the course run by the Luperci in his own day.[120] Yet, the Luperci, in returning to the cave for the feast, may well have encircled the hill instead of going back by the same route. In that act however, we do not see the ceremonial significance which attached in later times to the encircling of the Palatine, when the Luperci by their goat-skin thongs assured productivity to the women of Rome.

A ritualistic flight, we have seen, was a frequent and significant feature of expiatory rites. The details of the Lupercalia correspond to the other ceremonies of that type which have already been examined.[121] As they fled, the Luperci were pelted with missiles, just as were the priests who sacrificed the calf at Tenedos.[122] The Lupercalia culminated in a feast which is paralleled by the one served to the boys in the Stepteria when they were returning from their exile.[123] An expiatory sacrifice is the most frequent type in the worship of a god who is embodied in a dangerous animal like the wolf.[124] Therefore we may explain the Lupercalia in its earliest form as follows. The Luperci endeavored to avert from the people the deity's malignant power by offering it sacrifice. They sought to share the mysterious potency of the sacrificial animal by eating of its entrails. Yet they felt that the act of slaying an animal consecrated to the god was a sacrilege; therefore they fled, as from a crime, and expiated their guilt by being stoned. Having been thus purified, they returned to the Lupercal, and ate in sacramental fashion the flesh of the sacrifice. The mystic significance of the stoning and the sacramental nature of the meal is shown by the refusal of the Fabii to share those rites with the Quintilii.

Such a ceremony was naturally regarded by ancient scholars

as a Roman double of the Lycaea. In each festival the sacrifice was expiatory, being offered to appease a wolf-god. The priests incurred guilt by slaying the victim, and fled. After a purificatory experience they returned. In details the ritualistic acts of the two festivals were different, but the underlying meaning was the same.

This likeness between the festivals has caused some authorities to go still further, and to hold that the original sacrifice at the Lupercalia was a human being.[125] If that were so, it is very strange that there are no legends, as about the Lycaea, reminiscent of a loathsome rite. The story of human sacrifice that was connected with the cult of Valeria Luperca makes more noticeable the fact that, among the numerous legends of the Lupercalia, not one has the least suggestion that a human being was once the victim. Yet that is a thing that makes a deep impression, and is more liable than any other ritual act to produce a tale. Also, the rites of the Lupercalia fail to suggest an earlier slaughter of a man. If, for example, a man's blood is sprinkled upon the altar,[126] the symbolism is clear: the deity, being deprived of his accustomed sacrifice, receives in substitution a few drops of blood. Also, if the sword were placed at the throat of the young men, it would be emblematic of their death. Such a rite was performed at Halae in memory of an earlier human sacrifice, the priest going so far in his realism as to draw blood from the man's throat.[127] But the placing of the sword against the foreheads of the youths is certainly not a natural pantomime of sacrificial slaughter. The ritual of the Lupercalia involved also the wiping away of the blood by wool dipped in milk. That act, which is difficult to explain on the theory of human sacrifice, is, as we shall see,[128] an essential part of the blood-ceremony as explained upon another basis.

The parallelism between Lupercus and Lycaeus suggests another possible victim that was appropriate for a wolf-god, that is, a wolf.[129] But, if wild animals were ever sacrificed in Italy, not a vestige of such a rite has come down to us. Hence it is unsafe to assume that at some remote time a wolf was the sacrificial victim of the Lupercalia.

In the examination of the goat-cults of Greece,[130] we shall see that a human or a wild animal victim was often replaced in later times by a goat. It is possible that such a substitution took place in the Lupercalia in very early days, though the lack of evidence makes it safer to accept the goat as the original sacrifice. Dr. Farnell shows that the theory of sacramental union with a deity through sacrifice does not demand the belief that the deity was incarnate in the sacrificial animal.[131] He notes that in the Thesmophoria pigs were cast into a chasm, and devoured by snakes that seem to have been the embodiment of the earth-deity. In the same way a goat may well have been sacrificed to the chthonic wolf. Various instances of goat-sacrifice show that, even when the goat had not the character of an animal-god, it was a sacrificial victim that possessed a special sanctity.[132]

When the ancients called the Lupercalia a Pelasgian rite, and made Lupercus a double of Lycaeus, they were telling the truth. Those gods were the Greek and the Roman expression respectively of the same power. Both were evolved by huntsmen or by primitive shepherds, who shaped their deity in the form in which super human might was most clearly manifested to them. As in Asia Minor this power was incorporate in the lion, and in Crete in the bull, so in Arcadia and in Italy the wolf, which was the animal most numerous and most dreaded, was accepted as the embodiment of the god. He was a pitiless creature, whose baleful power both Pelasgians and Ligurians sought to avert by rites of expiation.

NOTES

1. Keller, *Thiere des klassischen Alterthums,* i, 159, 163; Preller, *Romische Mythologie,* i, u6; Reinach, *Orpheus,* 97.
2. See p. 36 O.M.
3. Verg., *Aen.,* 1 l. 785; Plin., *N. H.,* 7. 19. Strabo alone (5. 9. p. 226) ascribes this rite to Feronia, who had her shrine at the foot of Mount Soracte.
4. Deecke, *Die Falisker,* 4, 53; Preller, i, 268.
5. Farnell, v, 375-6, 388-90; Rhys, 638.
6. Serv. ad Verg., *Aen.,* I l. 785.
7. This is the suggestion of Dr. Jordan *(Kritische Beiträge,*163).
8. Dr. Mannhardt *(Wald- und Feldkult,* ii, 342) notes this similarity, though he believes that the festivals celebrated the summer solstice.·
9. Wissowa, *Religion und Kultus der Römer,* 238; Reinach, *Cultes,* i, 296; Deecke, 92-4.
10. Verg., *Aen.,* II 785; Plin., 7. 19; Solin., 2. 26.
11. Ad Verg., *Aen.,* I l. 785. Hades, who was very similar to Dis (Cook, *Zeus,* 99) at times wore a wolf-skin helmet. (See p. 28 n. 53.)
12. Plin., *N. H.,* 7. 19; Solin., 2.26.
13. Muller, *Die Etrusker,* ii, 68; Deecke, 94-5; Keller, *Thiere Kl. Alt.,* i, 172; Mannhardt, *W. F. K.,*327.
14. Modestov,229.
15. Paul. ex Fest.,106.
16. The Hirpi Sarani should not be confused with the Sabellian t ribe, the Hirpini, who journeyed to Southern Samnium under the guidance of a wolf (Strab., 4.12).
17. Modestov, 31.
18. Montelius, *La civilisation primitive en Italie,* ii, Pl. 307-331; Deecke,34.
19. Dionys., I. 21; Strab., 5. 9.
20. Dionys., I. 21. See also E. H. Bunbury, in Smith, *Diet. Geogr.,* i, 891.
21. Pseud. Plut. *Parallel.,* 35.
22. Farnell, ii, 441; Stoll, in Roscher, ii, 304.
23. See pp. 36-7 O.M.
24. Babelon, *Monnaies de la république romaine,* ii, 515-21.
25. See p.6 O.M.

26. The double name Valeria Luperca cannot have been the ancient form, therefore the adjective Valeria must be a later addition (Mommsen, *Römische Forschungen*, i, 5).
27. Roscher, ii, 2437.
28. Roscher, ii, 2385-95.
29. Wissowa, *R. K.*, 141; Mommsen, *The History of Rome*, i, 175; Preller, i, II5, 333.
30. *Lex.* ii, art. *Mars*. See especially 2399-2415.
31. *R. F.*, 34-5. In harmony with this view are Roscher, ii, 2429-34; Schwegler, *Römische Geschichte*, i, 228-315; De Sanctis, *Storia dei Romani*, i, 268--9; Preller, i, 332-46; Frazer, ix, 229-34; Piganiol,115.
32. *C. I. L.*, ii, 787r.
33. *C. I. L.*, ii, 7862. For these two Ligurian deities, see also Conway, *Ligurian Religion*, in Hastings, *Ency. Rel.*, viii, 69.
34. Paul. ex Fest., 106.
35. Liv., 1. 5.
36. Modestov, 24.
37. Peet, 32. See also Osborn, *Men of the Old Stone Age*, 434.
38. Modestov, 2,3.
39. Modestov, 252-5.
40. Var., *L. L.*, 5. 42, 53, IOI ; Verg., *Aen.*, 8. 51-6, 97; Liv., l. 7. 8; Dionys., r. 9, 22, 39,40; 2. r; Fest., 321; Serv. ad Verg., *Aen.*, l. 273; 3. 500 ; 7. 795; 8. 51; II. 317; Salin., r. 13; Macr ., l. 7. 30; II. 48.
41. Dionys., 2. I. I, 2.
42. Var., *R. R.*, 2. II. 5.
43. Lippert, ii, 549·
44. For a survey of the ancient cults of the Aventine and of the valley at its foot, see Merlin, *L'Aventin dans l'antiquité*, 45-52.
45. Verg., *Aen.*, 8. 230; Ov., *Fast.*, r. 551; 6. 82; Liv., r. 7.
46. Liv., I, II; Dionys., 2. 38, 40.
47. Macr., 1. 8. 2.
48. Dionys., I.32; Serv. ad Verg., *Aen.*, 8.337; Im., I.13.
49. Modestov, 252; Gilbert, *Geschichte und Topographie der Stadt Rome im Altertum*, I. 67.
50. Dionys., 1. 32. 4, 5; I. 79. 8.
51. Smith, *Semites*, 151; Jevons, *An Introduction to the History of Religion*, Gilbert (i, 53-7) notes the evidences of an ancient cult center on the Cermalus. Lippert (ii, 564) ascribes the cult at the Lupercal to the pre-Roman inhabitants of the Palatine.
52. *J. H. S.*, xxi, 129.
53. Dionys., 1. 79.
54. Verg., *Aen.*, 8. 630; Liv., 1. 5; Plut., *Rom.*, 2. 4; id. *de Fort. Rom.*, 8. D, E ; id. *Q. R.*, 21; Serv. ad Verg., *Aen.*, 8. 343; Just., 43. 2. 7; Arnob., *adv. Gent.*, 4. 3.
55. See p.25 O.M.
56. Dr. Pais, in an elaborate study, advances the view that the wolf in Italy was the animal incarnation of the earth-spirit *(Ancient Legends of Roman History*, 60, 95). See also Reinach, *Cultes*, 1,295.
57. Liv., 1. 4. 7.

58. Plut., *Rom.*, 5. 4.

59. *Anc. Leg.*, 46--95. This interpretation of Acea Larentia is supported by many authorities: Preller, i, 398-400, ii, 26; Lippert, ii, 547; Fowler, *R. F.*, 74.

60. *Anc. Leg.*, 84.

61. Just., 43· l. 7.

62. Ad Verg., *Aen.*, 8. 343.

63. This etymology is favored by Walde (447), by Marquardt *(Römische Staatsverwaltung*, iii, 439 n. 4), by Deubner *(Arch.f. Rel.* vol. xiii, 484), and by Lippert (ii, 564). The suggestion of Unger *(Die Lupercalien*, in *Rhein. Mus.*, vol.xxxvi, 64) that Lupercus comes from *lues* and *parco* has won no acceptance (Marquardt, iii, 438 n. lO; Gilbert, i, 145 n. 2; Freiler, i, 380 n. 4).

64. For this reason Schwegler suggests the etymology *lupus + hircus, wolfgoats,* saying (i, 361) that the two bands of the Luperci represent respectively the animal daemons, the wolf and the goat. This etymology is accepted unreservedly by Mannhardt *(Mythologische Forschungen*, 90), and tentatively by Hild (Daremberg-Saglio, iii,1399).

65. *Fast.*, 2. 421.

66. Lact., *Inst.*, l. 20. 1.

67. Ap. Arnob., 4.3.

68. Fowler, *R. F.*,312.

69. Jordan *(Krit. Beitr.*, 164-5) believes that *Luperca* was merely an expanded form of *lupa*, being developed from it on the analogy of *noverca*, and thus meaning nothing more than *wolf*. This view is supported by Otto (in Pauly Wissowa, vi, 2055), by Preller (i, 380 n. 4), by Gilbert (i, 145 n. 2), and by Mommsen *(H. R.*, i, 156). Walde, however (447), does not consider it probable, in view of the form of the word.

70. Hesych., Λυκοκτόνος.

71. *Hom. Hym. in A pol.*,373.

72. *Hym. orph.*, 33. 4.

73. *Cybele*, 7.

74. Strab., 8. 528.

75. Etymol. Mag.,Ἐλαφηβολίων.

76. Reinach, *Cultes*, i, 58; Aust, *Die Religion der Römer*, 4; Fowler, *R. E.*, 163.

77. Dr. Cook *(Zeus* 441-4) cites a number of instances in which the worshippers took the name of an animal-god.

78. Eur., *Bae.*, 83; Phot ., *Lex.*, *s.v.*

79. Just., 43. 1. 7.

80. See p.24 O.M.

81. Pan or Pan Lycaeus is named the god of the Lupercalia in the following passages: Verg., *Aen.*, 8. 344; Dionys., 1. 32. 3; Plut., *Q. R.*, 68; Serv. ad Verg., *Aen.*, 8. 343, 663; Charis., *Gram. Lat.*, i, 550. 10; Anton ., *Gram. Lat.*, v, 500.35.

82. *Fast.*, 2. 267-79.

83. *Fast.*, 2. 423.

84. The other reasons which have led persons to regard Faunus as the god of the Lupercalia are considered on pp.54-7 O.M.

85. Liv., 1. 5. 2.
86. Ad Verg., *Georg.*, 1. 10 . See also Serv. ad Verg., *Aen.* , 6. 775, and Cledon., *Gram. Lat.,v,35.*
87. *Fast.*, 2. 281.
88. Dionys., I. So; Ov., *Fast.*, 2. 279; Liv., I. 5. I , *2;* Plut., *Rom.*, 21; id. *Caes.*, 61; Serv. ad Verg., *Aen.*, 8. 343. See also Nilsson, 444 n. 2.
89. Dionys., 1. 11, 13, *22 ;* 2. 1; Pherec.fr. 85; Strab., 6. 3. 8.
90. See p.10 O.M.
91. Evander was regarded as the founder of the Lupercalia by Fabius Pictor, Cincius Alimentus, Cato, and Calpurnius Piso (Dionys., 1. 79). See also Liv., I. 5; Verg., *Aen.*, 8. 344. Acilius Glabrio followed the common Roman fashion of making Romulus the founder of Roman institutions: before Rome was established, he says (ap. Plut., *Rom* . 21), Romulus, having had his cattle stolen, sacrificed a goat and pursued the thieves; the Lupercalia commemorates that race.Variants of this account tell that Romulus and Remus, after they had conquered Amulius (Plut., *Rom.*, 21), or after Kumitor had given them permission to found a new city (Val. Max., 2.2.9), ran in joy to the place where they had been reared. All these accounts harmonize with those that ascribe the festival to Evander, in the vital point that the Lupercalia was established *before* the city of Rome was founded.
92. Paul. ex Fest., 87. The Julian Luperci, who were not added until Caesar's day (Dio Cass., 44. 6) need not concern us here.
93. Ov., *Fast.*, 2. 378; Aurel. Viet., *Or. Gent. Rom.*, 22.
94. Plut., *Fab. Max.*, I; Sil. It., *2.* 3; 6. 634; Paul. ex Fest., 87.
95. Friedlander, *Herakles,* 163, *et passim.*
96. Var., *L. L.*, 6. 82.
97. Durbach, in Daremberg-Saglio, iii, 80; Friedlander, 163-4. 98. Gruppe, 453-60.
99. Friedlander, 139.
100. Liv., I. 5.
101. Sil. Ital., *2.* 3. 102. Var., *L. L.*, 5. 45.
103. See pp. 61-3.
104. For the discussion of these elements, see chapters VIII, IX.
105. Var., *L. L.*, 5. 85.
106. Ovid *(Fast.*, 2. 361) names a *capella* as the victim. Plutarch *(Rom.*, 21) and Valerius Maximus (2. 2. 9) say that *goats* were slain. Servius alone (ad Verg., *Aen.*, 8. 343) names a *male goat* as the only victim.
107. Tubero alone speaks of them as wearing girdles cut from the skins of the goats (Dionys., I. So). These girdles seem to belong naturally with the goat-skin thongs which the Luperci carried at a later time. All the legends explain the nakedness of Romulus and Remus as due to their haste in running. It is unreasonable to imagine them, when in such haste, stopping to cut girdles. Dr. Deubner believes that the Luperci were in earliest times wholly naked, though he bases his conclusion on different grounds *(Arch.f. Rel.*, vol. xiii, 491-2).
108. Valerius Maximus alone (2. 2. 9) places the feast before the race.
109. *Fast.*, 2. 361,371.

110. See p. *22.*
111. Ov., *Fast., 2.* 371; Val. Max., *2. 2.* 9; Prudent., *contraSym., 2.* 862; Aurel. Viet., *Or. Genl. Rom., 22.*
112. In the legends, the Fabii are regularly made the followers of Remus.
113. Dionys., 1. 80.
114. Ov., *Fast., 2.* 373-8.
115. Liv., I. 7. 13.
116. Prop., 4. 1. 26.
117. Plut., *Rom.,* 21; Serv. ad Verg., *Aen.,* 8. 343.
118. Dr. Deubner cites instances of ceremonial nakedness *(A,ch. Rel.,* vol. xiii, 491).
119. Var., *L. L.,* 6. 34.
120. Plut., *Rom.,*21.
121. See p.23 O.M.
122. See p.23 O.M.
123. See p.23 O.M.
124. Toutain, in Daremberg-Saglio, iv.956.
125. Schwegler, i, 363. Others are cited by Marquardt, iii, 443, notesII-3.
126. Theophrastus (a p. Prophyr., *de Abst.,* 2. 27) notes an instance of thissort,
127. Eur., *Jph. Taur.,*1458.
128. See pp. 84-7 O.M.
129. See p.24) O.M.
130. See chap.V.
131. Farnell, iii, 90; id. *Sacrificial Communion,* in *Hibbert Jour.,* vol. iii, 319-21.
132. See p.51 O.M.

CHAPTER V

The Sacred Goat in Greece

THE VENERATION OF a wild animal tends to be crowded into the background as a people advances in civilization. When life becomes more settled, and savage beasts are no longer a constant menace, men are liable to embody their god in the form of one of the animals upon whom their existence largely depends: the ram, the bull, or the goat. In many cases this more kindly god absorbs, entirely or in part, the savage deity. In other instances the two gods exist side by side, but the cult of the savage god is modified by that of the more civilized one. The god of the pastoral stage who made his way most frequently into the cults of other deities was the goat-god. As the goat can thrive on the most barren hillside, his cult was widespread and important in Greece in very early times. In the Lupercalia the blows which were dealt by goat-skin thongs formed the most prom-inent feature of the ritual. To interpret this importance of the goat in a wolf festival, we turn to the cults of the goat in Greece.

In Crete the sacred goat was frequently portrayed by Minoan artists as a fertility fetish.[1] In later times it took the form of the goat Amaltheia, who expressed the general conception of the earthpower, being a giver of fertility and a protector from evil.[2] Her fertilizing potency came to be expressed in the cornucopia, which was probably developed from the original goat's horn, and which constantly appears in the possession of earth-deities, such as Hades, Gaia, or the river-gods.[3]

Pan was frankly a goat-god, not only in his half-human form,[4] but also in his instincts. As the goat was to the ancients the symbol of lust, so Pan was the incarnation of lustful passion.[5] He was, therefore, an embodiment of the creative and life-giving power of nature. Pan's cult originated in Arcadia, where Mount Lycaeus was sacred to him as well as to the wolf-god.[6] Thence his worship spread throughout the Greek world,[7] developing with particular strength among the Athenians.[8] Thus his character and the people who venerated him mark Pan as a Pelasgian deity.

Another primitive nature-god, Dionysus, was at times associated with the goat. Such titles as Ἐρίφιος, Μελάναιγις, or Αἰγίβολος,[9] also the myths in which Dionysus was disguised as a goat,[10] indicate that at times he was worshipped in goat-form. A legend of Potniae, in Boeotia, tells that the people, having offended Dionysus, were suffering from a frightful pestilence. In obedience to the Delphic oracle, a boy was sacrificed to the angry god; but not many years afterward Dionysus himself substituted a goat for the boy.[11] A goat was sometimes rent asunder in the wild orgy to Dionysus known as the Omophagia,[12] in which the worshippers devoured the raw flesh of a sacred animal and drank its blood, thus partaking of its divinity.[13]

Though Artemis was preëminently the goddess of the wild things, she bore the title Αἰγιναίας,[14] and among the Spartans and the

Athenians received a goat as her usual victim.[15] At her famous and ancient shrine at Brauron a curious rite was performed: maidens, known as *bears*, and wearing saffron robes which perhaps imitated a bear-skin,[16] danced a bear-dance in honor of the bear goddess Artemis, the ceremony ending with the sacrifice of a bear.[17] Yet in historical times a goat was usually sacrificed,[18] in substitution, evidently, for the wild-animal victim.[19] Another legend indicates that a human being was at one time sacrificed: the Athenians were said to have suffered from a pestilence because they had injured a bear, and a maiden was demanded in expiatory sacrifice; whereupon a man concealed his daughter, dressed a goat in her garments, and sacrificed it in her stead.[20]

Pan, Theodorus van Kessel, after Peter Paul Rubens, 1630 - 1660

The goat was important in the worship of Apollo, who was venerated in many places as a pastoral god.[21] In Crete legend told that a goat had suckled the twin sons of Apollo. A Cretan town, accordingly, sent to Delphi a bronze group of the goat and the babes as a votive offering.[22] At Delphi the Python, who was the first possessor of the oracular shrine, and who was slain by Apollo, was buried, we are told, by his son Αἴξ.[23] That seems to indicate that at Delphi the autochthonous serpent-cult was displaced by the goat-cult, and that, in turn, by the anthropomorphic deity. Goats were believed to have discovered the oracular cave at Delphi,[24] and were the usual sacrificial victims there. The oracle frequently enjoined upon its devotees the sacrifice of a goat.[25]

The magic power of the goat-skin, of such importance in the Lupercalia, was appropriated by some of the greater deities of Greece. Athena appears almost invariably wearing the goat-skin, the *aegis,* across her breast.[26] Apollo, Juno, and Zeus were also wearers of the *aegis,*[27] By putting on the skin of the goat, the anthropomorphic gods sought to transfer to themselves the power of the animal-god. The magic potency which the goat was supposed to possess is shown very clearly in a ceremony of Athens, in which a priestess bore a goat-skin to the homes of newly-married women.[28] This is naturally interpreted as being designed to secure offspring.[29] It offers, accordingly, an illuminating parallel to the use of the goat-skin in the Lupercalia.

As a sacrificial victim, the goat was used in various solemn rites, particularly in those of the expiatory type.[30] Thus a goat was sacrificed to Apollo Apotropaios at Marathon.[31] When the people of

Kleonae were threatened with pestilence, they sacrificed a goat at sunrise, and sent a bronze goat as a votive offering to Delphi.[32] In the Laconian ceremony of the *Κοπίδες,* the goat was the only animal that might be sacrificed, and the people ate its flesh in sacramental fashion, together with a certain kind of bread.[33] These instances of goat-sacrifice may well be parallel to that of the Lupercalia. There is no evidence in these rites that the goat was sacrificed as an animal-god; yet it was a victim that was especially potent to ward off evil.

Tempel of Apollo at Delphi, ca. 1915

In Greece the cult of the goat, which appeared in Minoan Crete, was centralized in Arcadia, and warmly welcomed in Athens and in Boeotia: that is, it was especially venerated among the Pelasgians. The goat was not an object of dread, as the wolf so often was, but was loved as the bringer of blessings—the life-giver. The goat was on friendly terms with other deities, sharing with Lycaeus his shrine, and being received at Delphi as the son of Python. As a sacrificial victim the goat was especially important. Often it seems to have been substituted for a wild animal or for a human being; at other times it had a magic potency to ward off evil. Even Olympian deities were influenced by the goat, for they were often glad to wear his skin, and thus to appropriate his creative power.

NOTES

1. Evans, *J. H. S.*, xxii, 182; Mackenzie, *Crete*, 188, 307; Fick, 147; Hogarth, *The Zakro Sealings*, in *J. H. S.*, vol. xxii, 1902, p. 34-7, Fig. 115-26 *et al.*
2. Callim., *Hym. in Iov.*, 48; Apollod., *Bibl.*, J. I. 7; Hygin., *Astr. Poet.*,13; Wernecke, in Pauly-Wissowa, i, 1721. The nursing of Zeus by Amaltheia is told only by Alexandrian writers, hence seems to have been a late development (Farnell, i,109).
3. Saglio, in Daremberg-Saglio, i, 220; Stoll, in Roscher, i, 263-5.
4. Wernicke, in Roscher, iii,1407.
5. Aug., *de Civ. Dei*, 15. 23; The Satyrs, of the same form and character as Pan, are to be recognized as merely the duplicates of Pan (E. Kuhnert, in Roscher, iv, 516-31; G. Nicole, in Daremberg-Saglio, iv, 1090.
6. See p.24 O.M.
7. Wernicke, in Roscher, iii, 1349-79.
8. Lucian, *Bis. Accus.*, 10; id., *Deor. Dial.*, 22.2.
9. Paus., 2. 35. 1; Hesych.,Ἐρίφιος; Schol. ad Aristoph., *Acharn.*,146.
10. Suid., Μελάναιγις Διόνσος; Ov., *Met.*, 5. 329; Apollod., *Bibl.*, 3. 4. 3.
11. Paus., 9. 8. 2.
12. Hesych., τραγηφόροι; Eur., *Bae.*, 139; Arnob., 5.19.
13. Harrison, 482.
14. Paus., 3. 14.2.
15. Ael., *Var. Hist.*, 2. 25; Xen., *Anab.*, 3. 2. 12, 13; id., *Hellen.*, 4. 2. 20; Plut., *Lycurg.*, 22.
16. Farnell, ii,437.
17. Aristoph., *Lysislr.*, 645, and Schol. *ad loc.*
18. Hesych., Βραυρωνίοις.
19. Farnell, ii,437.
20. Suid., Ἔμβαρος.
21. Farnell, iv, 123, 254.
22. Paus., 10. 16. 5.
23. Plut., *Q. G.*, 12.
24. Diodor., 16. 26. I, 2.
25. Diets, *Sibyllinische Blatter*, 51; Farnell, iv,254-5.
26. Diodor., 3. 70. 5; Farnell, i, 100.
27. Saglio, in Daremberg-Saglio, i, 101; Farnell, i,, 100, iv,255.
28. Suid., αἰγίς.
29. Farnell, i,100.
30. For a survey of the various cults in which the goat was a ceremonial victim, see Farnell, iv, 255.
31. Farnell, iv, 255.
32. Paus., 10. 11.5.
33. Athen., 138 f.

CHAPTER VI

The Sacred Goat in Italy

IN ITALY THE deities affiliated with the goat are far less numerous than in Greece. Outside the cult of the obscure Veiovis, of Faunus, and of Juno Caprotina, the goat plays only an insignificant part. Consequently the importance of the goat-skin as employed by the Luperci is the more remarkable. As we review the goat-cults of Italy, the question before us will be, "Did the cult of the goat in Italy have a similar history and significance to that which it had in Greece?"

The goat was sacrificed to Veiovis *ritu humano,* and the statue of Veiovis had a goat standing by his side.[1] The expression *ritu humano* is often taken to mean that an animal victim was substituted for a human sacrifice. If this is true, the sacrifice to Veiovis passed through the phases which we saw in the Greek cults. Very little is known about Veiovis, but he is regarded as unquestionably an underworld deity.[2]

A god having a far more intimate relation to the goat, and also much better known, was Faunus, an ancient deity of Latium, who is constantly mentioned with the aborigines of Italy.[3] The antiquity and character of Faunus comes out most clearly in his double, Fauna, the older deity, whom Faunus later displaced. She was known by many descriptive epithets: Fenta Fatua, Tellus, Ops, Maia, Bona Dea, or Dea Dia.[4] The kinship of this goddess to other earth-mothers was recognized by Macrobius, who considered her identical with Proserpina, Hecate, Semele, and Cybele.[5] She was, therefore, one of the numerous forms of the chthonic deity of the Mediterranean people.

Faunus was a god whose importance became shadowy as civilization advanced. The numerous legends of Faunus, god of oracles,[6] and mysterious creature of the wilds,[7] show how important a place he had in early days among the gods of Italy. But to the people of later times he lost much of his mystic power, and was merely a god of the herds. Out in the country districts sacrifice continued to be offered to him;[8] yet even there the almost total lack of votive inscriptions to Faunus shows how little real hold he had upon the people by the time writing was in general use.[9] Ultimately he came to be little more than a mythical king. Varro, in seeking to explain him, reversed the order of development, saying that Faunus belonged to the class of gods who, originally mortals, were deified after death.[10] This shows how vague he had become by Varro's day. Cicero says that he does not know at all what Faunus is.[11] In Rome Faunus won scant recognition; it was not until 194 B.C. that a temple was erected to him. Even then he was not admitted within the Pomoerium, but was established on the Tiber Island.[12] The temple once built, we hear nothing more of it.[13] Faunus owes most of his fame to the Alexandrian poets, who identified him with Pan.[14] Faunus is the god whom many modern scholars believe to have been the deity of the Lupercalia.[15] They explain his lack of a temple within the Pomoerium by saying that the Lupercal was his shrine.

The statue erected there, showing the god naked and girded with goat-skin,[16] they regard as a representation of Faunus. But the goat-skin girdle is not enough to show that Faunus was the deity portrayed. The artist who carved the image set up at the Lupercal, being obliged to represent a god who was but little known, met the difficulty by making him like the priests who bore his name. Justin makes this perfectly clear, for he states that the statue of Lupercus at the foot of the Palatine represented the god in the garb which the Luperci wore.[17]

Pan with sheeps and goats, Schelte Adamsz. Bolswert, after Jacob Jordaens, 1596 - 1659

Another reason which is offered for regarding Faunus as the god of the Lupercalia is that the temple of Faunus on the Tiber Island was dedicated February 13, two days before the Lupercalia.[18] This naturally seems to indicate a connection between the god and the festival; and it may, indeed, easily be true that the priests chose to associate this half-forgotten god, to whom they had just erected a temple, with a festival that was as ancient as he was, and in which the goat had a prominent part. Such syncretism is common enough in Roman religion. But this late association does not prove that Faunus was the original deity of the Lupercalia; and the common people seem never to have regarded him as such.[19]

In the country districts Faunus was not worshipped in February, but on the Nones of December, and in his rites there appears nothing that is a kin to the Lupercalia. A kid, an ewe, or a lamb was offered to him, then the shepherds danced in triple measure.[20] It was a cheery rustic celebration, directed toward the protection and the fecundity of the herds.[21] There was no suggestion of the lustral race and the life-giving blows by which the Luperci assured fertility and purification to human beings. In the cult of Fauna the offering of milk and the administering of blows [22] give a slight suggestion of the features of the Lupercalia. But milk was frequently used as a libation in early cults, and as an offering to Fauna it shows none of the mysticism which dominates its use in the Lupercalia. The blows were dealt by myrtle rods instead of by goat-skin thongs. It was, moreover, the statue of Fauna, not the worshippers, that was struck. The cult of neither Faunus nor Fauna, therefore, offers any basis for conecting Faunus with the Lupercalia.

Is there in the attributes of Faunus anything which might link him with that festival? Most frequently of all Faunus is spoken of as the god of prophecy and of oracles.[23] But there is not a suggestion of oracular inspiration in the Lupercalia. Very rarely Faunus is given the power of purifica tion,[24] but it seems to be too undeveloped in him to account for the significance of the Lupercalia as a lustral ceremony.

If Faunus was worhipped in the Lupercalia, it must have been because he was the god of the flocks.[25] This is the basis upon which many assume his connection with the ceremony, the race of the Luperci around the Palatine being regarded as a measure of protection for the cattle that in early times were herded there.[26] This view depends largely on the passage in which Servius says that Lupercus may be so named because he keeps the wolves from attacking the flocks.[27] As we have already seen,[28] this is merely an attempt to explain in the regulation hackneyed way the origin of the name Lupercus. A point deserving of more consideration is the statement of Gaius Acilius, that Romulus, when his cattle were stolen, invoked the aid of Faunus and ran forth naked in pursuit.[29] Possibly Acilius means to indicate by this that Faunus was the god of the festival. Acilius lived at the time when the temple of Faunus was built on the Tiber Island, and may have accepted the connection between Faunus and the Lupercalia which, it seems, the priests sought to establish. But if such was his view, it had little support; we hear no earlier suggestion of the sort, nor was it accepted by later writers.[30] But the words of Acilius do not necessarily point to Faunus as the god of the Lupercalia. He does not go on to say, as we might expect, that upon recovery of the cattle the Lupercalia was instituted in honor of

Faunus. He says, instead, that, because Romulus cast aside his garments to gain speed in running, the Luperci are now naked when they
race about the city. The point of the story, therefore, is to explain the
origin of the race and its ritualistic nakedness. Faunus seems to be
mentioned merely because he was a natural god to invoke in seeking
the lost cattle. The Lupercalia certainly must have meant more to
the people than a festival for the protection of the flocks. Centuries
after the urban populace of Rome had lost all interest in the raising
of cattle, the Lupercalia continued. The impassioned denunciation
of Pope Gelasius shows how vital it was as late as 450 A.D.[31]

As god of the herds and incarnate in the goat, Faunus, together with his doubles Incubo and Inuus,[32] was the giver of fertility.[33]
That is another reason frequently offered for associating him with
the Lupercalia. But there is no suggestion that Faunus gave to the
thongs carried by the Luperci their life-giving potency. That was due,
according to legend, to another deity of goat-form, Juno.[34]
Many scholars connect Faunus with the Lupercalia through the medium of Evander, whom they regard as a Hellenized Faunus, manufactured by ancient scholars to explain the existence in Rome of a
cult very like that of Lycaean Pan.[35] But Evander seems to be something more than a scholarly fabrication. He is strongly localized in
Arcadia, appearing in Tegea, in Parrhasion, in Pheneos, near Mess-
enia, and, most frequently of all, in Pallanteum, where there was in
the temple of Demeter a statue of Evander.[36] Thus Evander seems
to have been a local deity. His cult in Arcadia is believed to have
antedated Roman times.[37] The constant association of Evander with
Pan, and the belief that Evander, like Pan, was the son of Hermes,[38]

Goat, Dirk Dirksen, 1821 - 1885

indicates that he belonged to Pan's circle.[39] Evander may have been an obscure local god, later absorbed by Pan, or his name may have been a cult-title which attained a vague individuality. He was recognized by the Romans as a deity, for we hear of sacrifices offered to him and a shrine in his honor on the Aventine.[40] We must, therefore, account for Evander and his connection with the Lupercalia on other grounds than as a mere double of Faunus.

Evander seems to have been transplanted into Italy through the activity of Alexandrian scholars. When they had, identified Pan with Faunus, they rationalized Evander into the exile who established the cult of Pan, or, in other words, of Faunus, in Italy. In this way only was he known to the earliest annalists.[41] There we have the germ of the Evander legend.[42] Other details were soon added: Evander and his Arcadians offered an easy explanation of the Ligurians who had dwelt in the vicinity of Rome,[43] the chance likeness of the names Palatium and Pallanteum giving support to this idea. Consequently as early as Fabius Pictor we find the tale of Evander's hamlet on the Palatine.[44] Ultimately Evander was made to typify the whole stream of Greek civilization which, as early as the regal period, influenced Rome so profoundly. He was accordingly said to have been the one who had brought to the Romans the alphabet and the arts of civilization.[45] Pliny was content to say that the service was performed by the Pelasgians.[46] The mention of the alphabet draws our attention at once to Cumae, whence in all probability the knowledge of writing was brought to Rome. Furthermore, Evander was said to have imported the gods whom the traders of Cumae and of southern Italy introduced into Rome in early days, Heracles, Demeter, Hermes,

Castor and Pollux.[47] The tale that Evander was guided to Rome by Apollo [48] points again to Cumae, the seat of Apollo's worship, and the active force in the Hellenizing of Roman religion. Evander is the poetic figure typifying that activity.[49]

Ancient scholars went still further and made Evander the founder of certain Roman cults, those of Victory, Consus, and Carmenta. The latter, ancient Roman goddess though she was, was made the mother of Arcadian Evander.[50] Once recognized as the bringer of ancient cults, Evander almost inevitably became the founder of the Lupercalia, akin as it was to the Arcadian Lycaea.[51] But Evander was said to have established the Lupercalia, not because he was a double of Faunus, but because he wished to honor his native god Pan Lycaeus. All the writers make this explicit.[52]

We do not find, therefore, in the cult or the attributes of Faunus, nor yet in his connection with Evander, a valid reason for accepting him as the god of the Lupercalia.

The goat-Juno had a far more vital association with the Lupercalia than had Faunus: She, like Faunus, was primarily the giver of fertility. But she was honored by cults which offered a marked correspondence to the Lupercalia, and she was even connected with that festival by legend and by title.[53] In the study of Juno, therefore, we shall seek an explanation of the goat-element in the Lupercalia.

Very significant for our purpose is the cult of Juno Sospita, of Lanuvium. That town, which was devoted to a religion of the most ancient type, venerated Juno Sospita as the oldest of all its deities. Her cult was, in fact, the most famous of all the Juno-cults in Latium.[54] Juno Sospita was a warrior goddess, as was the earth mother of Crete.[55] The goat regularly furnished a part of Juno's martial equipment; the head, with the horns still attached, formed her helmet, and the skin fell down her back, or sometimes over her breast like the *aegis* worn by Athena.[66] We may naturally believe that the goat-skin endowed Juno with its magic power of protection from harm. This Juno of Lanuvium was said by Cicero to be distinctly different from the Roman Juno.[57] Her Ligurian origin is indicated by her bearing the figure-eight shield, a form which is characteristically Mediterranean.[58]

It is for our purpose worthy of note that Juno Sospita was originally embodied in, or at least associated with, the serpent, a creature belonging to a still more ancient religious stratum than the goat. Constantly the goddess is attended by a serpent,[59] which, in a story told by Propertius, is all-important. The guardian of ancient Lanuvium, he says, was a serpent. Once a year a maiden descended trembling to the awesome cavern where the creature dwelt, and bore to it an offering of cakes. If the maid were unchaste, she was instantly devoured by the monster; but if she were pure, the serpent accepted and ate the gift which she brought, an act which was hailed by the farmers as the omen of a fruitful year.[60] This chthonic serpent, having oracular power, merciless, yet giving bountiful harvests, is a typical form of the Mediterranean earth deity, and must have been the oldest embodiment of Juno Sospita. The scene described by Propertius is portrayed on a coin which bears on the obverse the head of Juno wearing her goat-skin helmet,[61] thus showing the union of the two conceptions of the goddess.

Head of Juno Sospita; behind, serpent on staff (?)
Rev. Girl standing, facing serpent.

The cult of Juno Sospita gives us a parallel of what may have occurred in the evolution of the Lupercalia. In the one festival the wolf, in the other the equally primitive serpent was worshipped; but as the goat-god gained influence among the shepherd folk of Latium, both wolf and serpent were thrust into the background. Juno Sospita arrogated to herself a share of the goat's power by wearing its skin; in the Lupercalia the priests of the wolf-god did the same, and also carried strips of the goat-skin, which conveyed to the people its magic potency. Thus in each case the goat-cult seems to have been grafted upon a more ancient worship.

The veneration of Juno Sospita became important in Rome when, at the close of the Latin War, Rome stipulated that she should share on equal terms in the cult at Lanuvium.[62] A temple to Juno Sospita was built in Rome in 194 B.C., the same year in which temples were dedicated to two other goat-deities; Faunus and Veiovis.[63] This interest in the primitive goat-gods is characteristic of that period, for during the war with Hannibal and the years immediately afterward the terror of the people caused them to turn to many chthonic gods as a means of succor.[64]

Rome itself was the site of another goat-cult, that of Juno Caprotina. In her ritual the element of blows was very prominent. As the blows dealt by the Luperci were the most noted feature of the Lupercalia, we shall, before beginning the study of Juno Caprotina, examine the use of blows in other cults of Greece and of Rome.

In Greece the religious stratum to which that rite belongs is shown by the fact that Arcadia affords the greatest number of instances.[65] A detailed study of the use of blows has been made by Dr. Mannhardt;[65] he cites numerous cases in which the blows, being directed against a person or a statue which represents either a deity or some power of fertility or of evil, are designed to drive out evil or to rouse the latent power of a god by freeing him from some nullifying influence. Though similar to the blows which smote the statue of Fauna,[66] they are not typical of those delivered in the Lupercalia, where it was the worshippers who were struck. Other rites afford a closer parallel: at an Arcadian festival to Dionysus the women celebrating it were smitten;[67] at another Arcadian ceremony, in honor of Demeter, the worshippers struck one another with twisted bark;[68] the mysteries of Eleusis included, as a means of purification, a mock fight in which the celebrants hurled stones at one another;[69] and the Spartans, in honor of Artemis Orthia, practiced a rite in which youths often died under the lash.[70] The deities of all these ceremonies were chthonic. In every case, Professor Reinach believes, the blows served to purify the worshipper and to act as a fertility-charm.[71]

We are now ready to interpret the ritualistic significance of the blows in the festival of Juno Caprotina, which occurred on the Nones of July. At the Caprae Palus, in the Campus Martius, the women of Latium, together with the female slaves, exchanged taunts and threw stones at one another in a sort of mock battle. Then, under a wild fig-tree—or goat-fig, the *caprificus*—they feasted and paid homage to Juno Caprotina, offering her the milky juice of the tree.[72] Varro says that they cut branches from this tree,[73] a statement which it is tempting to associate with the sham battle, as indicating that the women belabored one another with these switches as a fertility charm.[74] We have no direct statement to this effect; yet the prominence in the ceremony of the goat and the *caprificus*, which was also an emblem of fertility,[75] give us good reason to believe that the purpose of the rite was to increase productivity.

Preliminary to this festival was the Poplifugia, which occurred either on the same day or two days earlier.[76] Its distinctive feature was a hasty and disorderly flight of the people away from the Caprae Palus.[77] Legend told, in explanation of this rite, that, when Romulus was holding a *lustratio* of the citizens, he disappeared during a sudden storm, and the people fled in terror.[78] Following the suggestion of this legend, Schwegler interpreted the Poplifugia as a lustral rite.[79] This view has won considerable favor.[80] As a lustral, or expiatory ceremony, the Poplifugia is wholly intelligible. Dr. Fowler compares it with the Bouphonia, which we have already examined,[81] and conjectures that the priest and the people at Rome may have fled after some similar sacrifice, and for the same reason. Such, a rite, he notes, was especially appropriate in July, at the beginning of the unhealthy season, when the people were seeking to protect themselves from evil powers.[82] That protection gained, they were ready to receive the gift of fertility by the celebration of the Caprotine Nones.

If this interpretation is correct, the Poplifugia and Nonae Caprotinae are similar to the Lupercalia both in meaning and in ritual acts.[83] Each festival occurred at a time of year when the powers of evil were abroad; each had a ritual flight and blows as a prominent feature. At the Lupercalia was sacrificed a goat, which was the sacred animal of Juno Caprotina. The rite of the Nonae Caprotinae was celebrated under a *caprificus;* and hard by the Lupercal was another ancient and venerated fig-tree, the *Ficus Ruminalis.*

Is it possible that any of the cult acts of the Lupercalia were suggested by the ancient festival of Juno at the Caprae Palus? According to the legends, the blows of the goat-skin did not become a part of the Lupercalia until after the Romans had united with the Sabines, when an addition was made to the ceremony under the influence of Juno Lucina. She, like Juno Caprotina, was a goddess of fecundity.[84] Her sacred grove on the Esquiline was one of the oldest and most venerated shrines in the whole city.[85] To this grove, Ovid says, Romulus and his people repaired for help when their Sabine wives proved unfruitful. As they bent in supplication before the shrine, there came from the depths of the forest the strange words, "Let the sacred goat enter into the Italian women." Thereupon an Etruscan augur slew a goat, cut the hide into pieces, and bade the women submit to blows from the strips. Thus their curse of barrenness was removed, and thanks were given to Juno Lucina.[86] To have any point, this story must be based upon cult-practices, or at least upon a recollection of them, employed at the shrine of Juno Lucina. Evidently she had availed herself, as did her sister of Lanuvium, of the life giving power of the goat-skin, and by blows from it assured to her devotees the hope of children.

Ovid tells this story at the conclusion of his account of the Lupercalia, in which, by a series of questions, he clearly suggests the development of the festival. He begins, "Tell me, ye Muses, what was the origin of this sacred rite?" and replies that it was founded by Evander in honor of Pan.[87] Ovid then inquires what caused the race: "Why do the Luperci run naked?" and tells in answer the story of Romulus and Remus pursuing the lost cattle.[88] He then explains the names Lupercal and Lupercalia by telling of the rescue of Rumulus and Remus by the wolf.[89] About the rite of the blows, Ovid says to a young wife: "Oh bride, why are you waiting? Not by potent herbs, nor by prayers, nor by magic incantations shall you become a mother. Receive with patience the blows of the fecund hide, and your husband's father shall become a grandsire."[90] Thus Ovid introduces the fourth point in his description of the Lupercalia—the use and the power of the goat-skin. He explains that point by telling the story given above of Romulus's visit to the shrine of Juno Lucina. In this tale, Ovid follows the same version as Livy and Servius, who also state that Romulus initiated the rite of blows in order to free the Sabine women from barrenness.[91]

As the narration of an actual fact; Ovid's tale is worthless; but as an indication of kinship between the festivals of Juno and the

Lupercalia, and of a possible early transference of cult-practices, it is illuminating. It is in accord with what we have seen in Greek religion that the cult of the wolf-god should have been in time partially overlaid by the ritual of the goat-god. Since the Lupercalia and the ceremonials of Juno had, as we have seen, many points of likeness, it would have been very natural for the Romans to seek to make their goat-sacrifice more potent by adding to it the practices of the near-by shrines of Juno.

If such was the development of the festival, the change did not obliterate the original ceremonial, but brought into more direct contact with the people the potency of the sacrificial goat: the Luperci now wore girdles cut from the skin of the victim, and carried in their hands strips of the same skin, with which they smote the women.[92] Hence their race about the city no longer seemed a lustral flight, but a means of carrying fertility to the people. The old ceremonial was thus overlaid by the new ritual. The ancient cult-acts continued, but their meaning was largely changed.[93]

The fundamental character of Juno would have made it very natural for her to win a place in the Lupercalia, for she was in essence and in origin closely akin to Luperca. Juno was, Varro tells us,[94] "the earth," hence she was merely another form-of that chthonic power which was also embodied in the wolf. But, whereas the wolf early sank to a secondary role, Juno became highly honored through the whole of central Italy, and, in her triumphant progress, must have assimilated many deities like herself, but less powerful. Such was the fate of Valeria Luperca. Juno's invasion of the Lupercalia, therefore, is merely a characteristic incident of her career. The month in which the Lupercalia was celebrated, February, was sacred to the chthonic gods,[95] among others, to Juno.[96] Juno was also associated with February, the month of purification, by her title of *Februata*, "the Purifier".[97] The goat-skin thongs with which the Luperci gave fertility to the people were also thought of as a means of purification, and were called *amicula Junonis*.[98] That name, surely, gives the clearest possible evidence of Juno's place in the Lupercalia. Yet many scholars are content to say that the thongs were so named because the festival was of especial concern to women, and that Juno was a goddess of women. Paulus leaves room for no such vague connection as that. He says out right that the Lupercalia was the festival of Juno Februata.[98]

When searching for a possible connection of Faunus with the Lupercalia, we found nothing in the legends concerning that god, in his cult, or in his character, which was significant enough to allow us to associate with him the goat element of the Lupercalia. In the case of Juno, on the contrary, legend attributed to her command the blows with the goat-skin, and the thongs were called "Juno's thongs". The Lupercalia was the most important purificatory rite among the Romans, and Juno, with the title Februata, was a goddess of purification. The month in which the Lupercalia occurred was sacred to Juno, and the Lupercalia itself was called Juno's festival. Upon this evidence, we conclude that Juno won for herself a place in the ritual of Lupercus , and grafted upon that ancient rite a ceremony that was distinctively her own.

The goat-deities in Italy seem to have been a product of the Ligurians, and played a role similar to that of the Pelasgian goat-gods. In each country the ritual of the goat often found a place in other cults, and imprinted its own peculiar stamp upon t hem. Thus it influenced the Lupercalia, which, in its original form as a rite to the wolf-deity, was apotropaic, being designed to ward off the powers of evil, and emphasizing the negative power of the earth-spirit. The goat-god, on the other hand, was especially the giver of fertility; hence his cult stressed the positive side of the earth-spirit. Therefore with the incorporation into the Lupercalia of the goat's fructifying power, the festival had a twofold function: to protect the people from evil, and to set free the forces of fertility.

NOTES
1. Ov., *Fast.,* 3. 443; Gell., 5. 12. 12.
2. Wissowa, *R. K.,*238.
3. Dionys., 1-. 43; Suet., *Vitell.,* I. 1; Gell., 5. 21. 7; Serv. ad Verg., *Aen.,*8. 314.
4. Dr. Pais *(Anc. Leg.,* 63-80) has shown in detail the identity of these deities.See also Fowler, *R.F.,* 74.
5. Macr., I. 12. 23, 24.
6. Verg., *Aen.,* 7. 81; Serv. ad Verg., *Aen.,* 7. 47, 81; Prob. ad Verg., *Georg.,* I. 10; Just., 43. I. 8; Isid., *Orig.,* 8. II. 87.
7. *Corp. Gloss.,* v, 198. 19, 20; Otto, in Pauly-Wissowa, vi,2058.
8. Prob. ad Verg., *Georg.,*1. 10. ·
9. Wissowa, *R. K.,* 213; Fowler, *R. F.,*258.
10. Ap. Serv. ad Verg., *Aen.,* 8.275.
11. *N. D.,* 3. 15.
12. Vitr., 3. 2. 3.
13. Fowler, *R. F.,*258.
14. Wernicke, in Roscher, iii,1407.
15. Schwegler, i, 232 n. 27; Preller, i, 380; Mommsen, *H. R.,* i, 208; Wissowa, *R. K.,* 210-12. Marquardt (iii, 439) identifies Lupercus with Faunus. Lupercus is regarded as an epithet of Faunus by Otto (in Pauly-Wissowa, vi, 2056), Roscher (i, 1455), and Hild (in Daremberg-Saglio, iii, 1399). Dr. Fowler, however, does not believe that Faunus was the deity of the Lupercalia (R. *F.,* 313, *Roman Ideas of Deity,* 94).
16. Just., 43. I. 7.
17. Just., 43. I. 7. Though Justin mentions Faunus in the sections immediately before

and immediately after the one cited, he speaks of him only as the king of Italy who welcomed Evander .

18. Ov., *Fast.,* 2. 193.
19. In this explanation, I have closely followed Dr. Warde Fowler (R.*F.,*258).
20. Hor., *Od.,* 3. 18, *omnis.*
21. Roscher, i, 1455.
22. Arnob., *adv. Genl.,* 5. 18; Lact., *de Fals. Relig. ,* I. 22. 1; *I, facr.,* I.12.25.
23. Vitr., 8. 3. 2; Verg., *Aen.,* 7. 81; Ov., *Fast.,* 4. 649-66; Plut., *Num.,*15; Prob. ad Verg., *Georg.,* 1. 10 ; Serv. ad Verg., *Aen.,* 7. 81; Isid., *Orig.,* 8. 11.87; *Corp. Gloss.,* v, 199. 15, 16.
24. Ov., *Fast.,* 3. 291; Plut., *Num.,* 15.
25. Porphyr. ad Hor., *Od.,* 3. 18.13.
26. See the authorities cited in note 15.
27. Serv. ad Verg., *Aen:,* 8.343.
28. See p.37 O.M.
29. Ap. Plut., *Rom.,*21.
30. Ovid's use of the name Faunus as the equivalent of Pan Lycaeus has already been considered (see p.38 O.M).
31. Gelas., *adv. Androm.,* in *Corp. Script. Eccles. Lat. ,* xxxv,453-64.
32. Wissowa, *R. K.,* 21r.
33. Rutil. Nam., 1. 234; Isid., *Orig.,* 8. 11. 103, 104; Hieron. ad *Is.,* I. 13. 21.
34. See p.61 O.M.
35. Marquardt, iii, 439; Preller, i, 387; Roscher, ii, 2822; Schwegler. i,354.
36. Verg., *Aen.,* 8. 51; Ov., *Fast.,* I. 545; Liv., I. 5. 1 ; 2. 1 3; Paus., 8. 43. 2; 8. 44. 5; Plut., *Philop.,* 18.
37. De Sanctis, *Storia dei Romani,* i,191.
38. Dionys., 2. I. 3; Paus., 8. 43. 2; Tzetzes, ad Lycoph., 772.
39. Robert, in Pauly-Wissowa , vi, 839-40.
40. Dionys., 1. 32. 2 .
41. Serv. ad Verg., *Georg.,* 1. 10.
42. Lübkers, *Reallexikon des klassischen Altertums,* 348; Fowler, *R.F., 258* n.1.
43. De Sanctis, i,192.
44. Dionys., 1. 79. See also 1. 31, 89.
45. Liv., 1. 7, 8; Dionys., 1. 33. 4; Tac., *Ann.,* 11. 14; Mar . Viet., *G. L.,* vi, 23. 14; vi, 194. 16.
46. *N. H.,* 7. 193.
47. Liv., 1. 7. 3; Verg., *Aen.,* 8. 102; Dionys., 1. 33; Fest., 269.
48. Verg., *Aen.,* 8. 336.
49. Schwegler, i, 359; Preller, ii, 341.
50. Liv., 1. 7. 8; Ov., *Fast.,* I. 479-500; Dionys., I. 32, 33; Paul. ex Fest ., 101.
51. See p. 46 n. 88 O.M.
52. Liv., 1. 5; Verg., *Aen.,* 8. 344; Dionys., 1. 79.
53. See p.61 O.M.
54. Ihm, in Roscher, ii, 595; Wissowa, *R. K.,*188.
55. Graillot,4.
56. Daremberg-Saglio, iii, Fig. 4185-88; Roscher, ii, Fig. on pp. 6o6-9.

57. *N. D.*, 1.*82*.
58. Daremberg-Saglio, iii, Fig. 4186, 4188; Mackenzie, *Crete,*159-60.
59. Daremberg-Saglio, iii, Fig. 4186, 4188; Roscher, ii, Fig. on pp. 6o8, 609.
60. Prop., 4. 8.3-14.
61. Daremberg-Saglio, iii, Fig. 4187.
62. Liv., 8. 14.
63. Liv., 32. 30. 10; 34. 53. 3·
64. For a survey of this period, see p.87-9 O.M.
65. Mannhardt, *Myth. Forsch.,*113-40.
66. See p.55 O.M.
67. Paus., 8. 23. 1.
68. Hesych., Μόροττον.
69 Mannhardt, *Myth. Forsch.,* 209.
70. Paus., 3. 16. 7.
71. *Cultes,* i, 180-3. This view is also expressed by Farnell, (v, 163), and by Jevons *(Hist. Rei.,* appendix to eh. 24).
72. Polem. Silv., *C. I. L.,* i, 269; Var., *L. L.,* 6. 18; Plut., *Rom.,* 29; id. *Cam.,* 33; Auson. *de Fer.,* 9; Macr., I. 11. 36, 40.
73. Var., *L. L.,* 6. 18.
74. Fowler, *R. F.,* 179; Frazer, ii,317.
75. Schwegler, i, 234; Frazer, ii,317.
76. Plut., *Rom.* , 29; Gilbert, i. 291; Hild, in Daremberg-Sag lio, iv, 579.
77. Var., *L. L.,* 6.18.
78. Liv., 1. 16; Dionys., 2. 56; Plut., *Rom.,* 29; id. *Cam.,* 33.
79. *R. G.,* i, 532-5.
80. It is accepted by Gilbert (i, 290), by Marquardt (iii, 325), and by Fowler (R. *F.,* 175-6).
81. See p. 23 O.M.
82. R. F., 176.
83. The similarity of ritual acts between these two festivals and the Lupercalia has been noted by Schwegler (i, 533), by Hild (in Daremberg-Saglio, iv, 579), and by Ihm (in Roscher, ii,599).
84. Hild, in Daremberg-Saglio, iii, 685,
85. Var., *L. L.,* 5. 49; Freiler, i, 273.
86. Ov., *Fast.,* 2.429-49.
87. *Fast.,* 2. 269-79.
88. *Fast.,* 2. 283-380. See also p. 46 n. 91 O.M.
89. *Fast.,* 2. 381-422.
90. *Fast.,* 2. 425.
91. Liv. ap. Gelas., *adv. Androm.,* 12; Serv; ad Verg., *Aen.,* 8.343.
92. Plutarch *(Rom.,* 21) and Valerius Maximus (2. 2. 9) say that the Luperci smote all whom they met. This may well have been the original practice; but, since the rite had especial significance for women, they were often thought of as the only celebrants.
93. It is quite possible that at this time the stoning of the Luperci (see pp.40,41 O.M.)

was discontinued. Since the race of the priests seems now directed wholly toward the gift of fertility, the act of stoning no longer has any point.

94. *L. L.*, 5. 65, 67.
95. Lyd., *de Mens.*, 4. 25; Macr., I. 13. 7; Solin., I. 40.
96. Lyd., *de Mens.*, 4. 25. Wissowa *(R. K.*, 185) remarks on the significance of the dedication days of Juno's temples, the one in the Forum Holitorium being dedicated on the first of February, and the one to Juno Lucina on the first of March. Wissowa considers it more than a coincidence that these two dedication days fell on the two Kalends that were nearest to the Lupercalia.
97. Paul. ex Fest., 85; Mart. Cap., 2.149.
98. Paul. ex Fest., 85.

CHAPTER VII

The Dog as Sacred Animal in Greece

ONE OF THE features of the Lupercalia which has aroused the greatest amount of scholarly speculation, is the use of a dog as sacrificial victim. Such a sacrifice was very unusual, both in Italy and in
Greece. A survey of the places in which it was employed and the
interpretation which was given to it, will assist us to understand its
significance in the Lupercalia.

Even in Pelasgian times the dog seems to have been venerated
as a sacred animal in certain parts of the Aegean world. Because of
the frequent occurrence of the figure of a dog on the hieroglyphic
seals of Crete, Sir Arthur Evans believes that the dog was sacred to
the Minoan goddess,[1] though it was one of the less important of the
many animals that were attached to her. At a later period the dog
made his way into the Cretan myths of Apollo.[2] Cydonia was said
to have been founded by a son of Apollo, Cydon, who, when a babe,
was suckled by a dog.[3] This legend was represented upon the coins
of Cydonia.' In Phaestos, too, the dog was associated with Apollo,[5]
and a dog appeared upon the coins of Phaestos.[5] Similarly, in Caria,
Apollo was said to have assumed the form of a dog when he begot

Telmissus.[7] The dog appears also in the later myths of Zeus, who was said to have been guarded in his infancy by a golden dog as well as by a goat.[8] In another account, the nurse of Zeus was named Cynosura.[9]

In Hellenic times, the deity who was most closely associated with the dog was Hecate,[10] of Thrace. Though the Thracians of historical times were probably Aryans, the early inhabitants of the land were Pelasgians.[11] They worshipped the characteristic earth-deity of the Pelasgians, and profoundly influenced the religion of the invaders.[12] Hecate was markedly chthonic,[13] and belonged undoubtedly to an ancient religious stratum.[14] In art and in literature Hecate is constantly represented as dog-shaped or as accompanied by a dog.[15] Her approach was heralded by the howling of a dog.[16] The dog was Hecate's regular sacrificial animal, and was often eaten in solemn-sacrament.[17]

Dog-fight with wolf, after Antonio Tempesta, ca. 1600 - 1630

Plutarch uses two words which give the dominant characteristics of Hecate: χθνία and ἀποτροπαία;[18] that is, she was a goddess of the underworld and of purification. At the crossroads, which were regularly sacred to gods of the lower regions, men sought communication with Hecate.[18] She had the souls of the dead under her especial charge,[19] and, as a natural result, was invoked by all who worked in magic and witchcraft.[20] Hecate's lustral power became operative chiefly through the sacrifice of a dog, which, Plutarch says, nearly all the Greeks employed as a means of purification.[18] Thus, in honor of Hecate, slain puppies were carried through a city, and were used to strike anyone who was in need of cleansing.[21] Among the Boeotians and the Macedonians a dog was cut asunder, and persons walked between the parts.[22]

Hecate was constantly identified by the Greeks with Artemis,[23] and was frequently grouped with Demeter and with other primitive powers of vegetation, such as Pan, Dionysus, Cybele, and Priapus. As goddess of the underworld, she was naturally associated with, or even identified with, Hades and Persephone.[24] The goddesses of women, Γενετυλλίς and Εἰλιονεία, were regarded as very similar to Hecate, and received a dog in sacrifice.[25] As a deity of purification, Hecate came to be honored in the Orphic Hymns beyond all other gods.[26] Ultimately the cult of Hecate spread throughout the Greek world.[27] Mysterious and alien goddess that she was, Hecate appealed to the imagination as one who could save men from every form of evil.

It was a natural sequence of the cult of Hecate, or, perhaps, an independent development of the same idea, that the dog became the animal in whose form the powers of the underworld especially appeared. In ancient times the dead were thought by the Greeks to visit the earth in the form of a serpent, but later they were believed to assume the shape of a dog as well.[28] The dæmon of Pestilence too, according to a legend, once disguised himself as an old beggar; but when the beggar had been stoned to death, it was a Molossian hound that lay in his place.[29] The same idea seems the basis of a celebration at Argos, in which on a certain day in the hot season men killed all the dogs that they met.[30] The fact that every dog that was seen was killed, indicates that they were not lustral offerings , but the personification of pestilence.

The dog was prominent in the cult of Aesculapius. Certain legends tell that when a babe he was rescued and suckled by a dog.[31] Statues and coins show him accompanied by a dog.[32] At the temples of Aesculapius, dogs were in attendance, and were believed to heal the sick by licking them with their tongues.[33] In Athens figurines of dogs were brought as votive offerings to the Asklepeium,[34] and a dog was said to have protected the treasures there from theft.[35]

The worship of Aesculapius originated in Thessaly, which at a very early date was overrun by bands from Thrace.[36] The oldest sites of the cult were in the original seats of the Lapiths, the Phleg-yae, and the Minyae,[37] who were all pre-Aryans.[38] Aesculapius was an earth-deity, as is shown by his oracular power, his healing art, and the cult-practices at his shrines.[39] In his cult, the power of the dog toward off evil, became limited to freeing people from disease.

In a few sporadic instances, other deities had the dog as a sacred animal. To the Thracian Ares dogs were sacrificed by the Car-ians and the Spartans.[40] In both these places the cult was a Thracian product. Caria was at one time overrun by Phrygians from Thrace, and the cult of Hecate was deep-rooted there.[41] Sparta seems to have gained the Ares cult from Boeotia, to which it was carried from Thrace in pre-Hellenic times.[42]

The Thracian cult of the dog spread even to Sicily. Its chief center there was in the north-western corner of the island, which, shortly after the fall of Troy, it seems, was colonized by the Elymians, who claimed descent from either the Trojans or the Phrygians. Dr. Freeman, after an acute analysis of the evidence about the origin of this people and of the modern theories concerning them, concludes that they probably came from Western Asia Minor, and that they were non-Hellenic, but had evidently been in early days closely connected with Hellas.[43] All this seems to class the Elymians as one of the Pelasgian peoples of Asia Minor.

Legend explained the Elymian settlements in Sicily by the story that when Troy, in the days of Laomedon, was harried by a sea monster, a certain Trojan sought to save his daughters from possible sacrifice to the monster by sending them to Sicily. When they arrived there they established, in gratitude, a temple on Mount Eryx to Aphrodite. This Aphrodite is called by Lycophron "the Zerynthian Mother."[44] Tzetzes explains that she was the Aphrodite of Thrace and Zerynthus, and that she had a sacred cave on Zerynthus.[45] Inasmuch as this island was famous as a seat of Hecate's worship, Dr. Freeman believes that the Zerynthian Aphrodite was merely another name for Hecate.[46] At any rate, the dog was sacred to Aphrodite of Eryx, for a coin issued by that city shows Aphrodite on one side and a hound on the other.[47]

Time of Tiberius, AD 14-37. Aphrodite standing left, holding dove / Wolf seated left, double axe behind; all within wreath.

The veneration which the Elymians had for the dog appears also in the legend that one of the exiled maidens, named Segesta, won the love of the Sicilian river-god Crimisus, and that he visited her in the form of a dog. By him she became the mother of Agestes, who founded the cities of Segesta, Eryx, and Entella.[48] This legend figured prominently on the coins of the Elymians. Of twenty-five coins of Segesta which are listed in the Hunterian collection, all except two represent the head of Segesta on one side and a dog on the other.[49] Sometimes the dog accompanies a youthful hunter. Both dog and hunter are interpreted as representations of the river Crimisus.[49] Other symbols that often appear on the coins are a wheel, a grain-plant, or a head of grain. The latter two seem to indicate that in Sicily the dog's apotropaic power was enlisted in the protection of the crops.[50]

The cult of the dog early appeared in the eastern part of Sicily as well as in the western. Coins of Syracuse, some of which were issued before 500 B.C., represent a dog.[51] One of them bears on one side the head of Apollo. This may easily be an echo of the Cretan association of the dog with Apollo,[52] since Syracuse had close connections with Crete, even in Minoan days.[53] At the foot of Mount Etna was the shrine of Adranos, where one thousand dogs were kept. They were the guardians of the temple, guiding and protecting righteous pilgrims, but driving off or killing the wicked.[54] Adranos is interpreted by Dr. Freeman as an ancient fire-god of the Siculi, and a natural product of the volcanic mountain.[55] There is nothing to indicate that Adranos was ever thought of as dog-shaped, nor was a dog sacrificed to him. The dog had, therefore, a less intimate place in his cult than in those of the Elymian deities, and was probably an Aegean importation which was grafted upon the cult of the Siculian god. By the days of Timoleon, Adranos was worshipped through all Sicily; accordingly, after the Mamertines overran North-Eastern Sicily, they frequently represented on their coins the head of Adranos and a dog.[56]

The cult of the dog was honored among the Pelasgians of Crete and of Thrace, but had its chief development in the latter place. From there is spread in pre-Hellenic days through Thessaly and Boeotia, and ultimately through the whole Greek peninsula. Asia Minor, too, was subjected to repeated waves of Thracian migration, so that there the cult of the dog came to be highly venerated. The Elymians, who came from Asia Minor, carried with them to Sicily the sacred dog, and established his worship in their new home. The dog was accepted as a sacrificial victim, Plutarch tells us,[57] by none of the

Olympian gods. To the Greeks the dog always remained an animal of uncanny power, which, when offered in sacrifice, had especial potency to purify and to ward off every form of evil.

NOTES

1. *Scr. Min.,* 208.
2. Whether this was due to the Minoan reverence of the dog as a sacred animal, or to the later spread of Hecate's cult to Crete, is immaterial for our purpose.
3. Stephanus, κυδωνία; Schol. ad Hom., *Odyss.,* 19. 176; Stoll, in Roscher, ii, 1674.
4. Head, *Historia Nummorum,* 391-2.
5. Gruppe, 1446.
6. Head, 402.
7. Suidas, Τελμισσεῖς.
8. Anton. Lib.,36.
9. Eratosth., 2.
10. The association of the dog with Hecate may have been due, wholly or in part, to the influence of Persia, where the dead were often left to be devoured by dogs (Herod., 1. 140), and were believed to be guided to the lower world by dogs (Liebrecht, 23; Gruppe, 407 n.1).
11. Wace and Thompson, *Prehistoric Thessaly,* 253; d'Arbois, *Les premiers habitants de l'Europe,* i, 90-7; Kretschmer, 173; Fick, 99; Farnell, ii, 507. L. J. Myres (*A History of the Pelasgian Theory, J. H. S.,* xxvii, 173) notes that in the Homeric catalogue of the ships the dominant folk between the Hebrus and the Hellespont were not Thracians, but Pelasgians. Herodotus (I. 57) speaks of a village in Thrace that was occupied by Pelasgians who, in his day, still spoke the Pelasgian language.
12. Tomaschek, *Die alten Thraker,* in *Sitzungsb. d. philos. hist. Cl. d. kais.Akad. d. Wissensch.,* Bd. cxxviii, Wien, 1893,1 12, 113; Hall, *N.E., 576;* Farnell, N.C.R., 29.
13. Hall, *O. C. G.* 297; Heckenbach, in Pauly-Wissowa, vii, 2773.
14. Rohde, ii.80.
15. Nonnus Dionysiacus, 3. 74; Eustath. ad Hom., *Odyss.,* p. 1714. 41; Farnell, ii, 508.
16. Theocr., 2. 35.
17. Plut., *Q. R.* 52, 68, I II ; Schol. adTheocr., 2.12; Porphyr.,de *Abst.* , *3* .17; Schol. d Aristoph., *Pax,* 276; Suidas, Ζηρυνθία Σαμοθράκη.
18. *Q. R.,* II I.
19. *Ety. Mag.,* 626. 44; Heckenbach, in Pauly-Wissowa, vii, 2778.
20. Hecate was the patron deity of the sorceress Medea (Ap. Rhod., 3. 841; Eur., *Med.* 395.See also, Rohde, ii, 75-87; Gruppe, 1272 n. 1.
21. Plut.,Q.R.,68,III.
22. Plut., *Q. R.,* 11I; Curt., 10. 9. 12.

23. Serv. ad *Verg., Aen.,* 4.511; Gruppe, 189; Heckenbach, in Pauly-Wissowa, vii, 2770.
24. Gruppe, 1291 n. 1; Heckenbach, in Pauly-Wissowa, vii, 2770-3;Farnell, ii, 512.
25. Plut., *Q. R.,* 52; Hesych. Γὲνετυλλίς.
26. Dieterich, *De hymnis orphicis,* 44.
27. Farnell, ii, 502-8.
28. Gruppe, 410, 803-4.The dog Cerberus seems to have been a late development that arose from the peculiar use of the word *dog* in the sense of *servant.* See Durbach, in Daremberg-Saglio, iii, 503; Immisch, in Roscher, ii, 1133.
29. Philostratus, *Apollonius of Tyana,* 4.10.
30. Ael., *N. A.,* 12. 34.
31. Paus., 2. 64. 4; Paul. ex Fest., 110; Lact., *Div. Inst.,* 1. 10. 1.
32. Paus., 2. 27. 2; Head, 369.
33. *Ath. Mitth.,* vol. xvii, 245. Deubner, *De incubatione,* 39. In Epidaurus the dog was largely replaced by the sacred animals of that region, the serpent and the goat (Paus., *2.* 26. 4; 2. 27. 2).
34. Martha, *Cat. Mus. Ath.* No. 169-71. 35. Ael., *N. H.,* 7.13.
35. Wace and Thompson, 232.
36. Thraemer, in Pauly-Wissowa, ii, 1643.
38. Hall, *N. E.,* 61. See p. 13 n.4.
39. Gruppe, 1448; Thraemer, in Roscher, i,626. Although Aesculapius appears in Homer, he seems to be a *hero* rather than a deity, for Homer always speaks of him as ἀμύμων (Thraemer, in Roscher, i,619).
40. Arnob., 4. 25.
41. Farnell, ii,5o6.
42. Farnell, v,403.
43. *History of Sicily,* i, 195-220, 542-59.
44. Lycophr., 958.
45. *Ad Lycophr.,* 449, 958.
46. *Hist. Sic.,* i.548.
47. Macdonald, *Catalogue of Greek Coins in the Hunterian Collection,* 181; Evans, *Ser. Min.,*208.
48. Lycophr., 961; Serv. ad Verg., *Aen.,* I. 550; 5.30.
49. *Hunterian Collection,* 212-16; Head, 165.
50. Coins of the Thracian Chersonese also represent a dog with a stalk of Larley behind him *(British M useum. Catalogue of Greek coins. Thrace,* 197).
51. *Hunterian Collection,* 235; Head, 180.
52. See p. 67 O.M.
53. Evans, *Scr. Min.,* 95.
54. Ael., *H. A.,* 11. 20; 11. 3.
55. *Hist.Sic.,* i, 183-8.
56. Head, 156.
57. *Q. R.,* III c.

CHAPTER VIII

The Dog as a Sacred Animal in Italy

AMONG THE ROMANS there was no clearly marked center of the cult of the dog, as there was in Greece. Moreover, details about the few dog-cults which are found in Italy are scanty. This makes an eluci-dation of the sacrifice of a dog in the Lupercalia very difficult, and we cannot hope to do more than offer a reasonable theory about its origin and significance, based upon a survey of the other dog-cults of Italy and of Greece.

The god Silvanus is constantly portrayed in art with a dog at his side.[1] Yet the dog had no part in the cult of Silvanus: there is no indication that Silvanus was ever thought to be of dog form; a dog was not sacrificed to him, nor did it appear in any of the legends about him. It seems probable, therefore, that the dog was attached to Silvanus because of an art convention: just as a dog was regularly represented with the huntress Diana, so Silvanus, the guardian of the boundaries of the cultivated land, was naturally accompanied by the watchfuldog.[2]

Dogs were able to see the Fauni.[3] This seems due to the wide spread belief in the uncanny power of the dog to discern either ghosts or a deity who was invisible to men.[4] There is nothing in the cult or the attributes of Faunus to indicate that the dog was sacred to him.

Most clearly marked of the cults of the dog was the sacrifice of a dog at the Robigalia. Robigus was the dreaded blight, or mildew, which attacked the grain while it was forming in the ear and caused it to turn black and wither.[5] Robigus was, therefore, a *numen* who must be placated in order to avert evil from the crops.[6] The Robigalia was established in early times [7] in order to ward off this destructive blight.[8] The rite being apotropaic, the dog sacrifice had the same significance that it had among the Greeks. We remember that on the coins of Sicily the dog often appeared in conjunction with a sheaf or an ear of grain,[9] so that there, too, it may have been thought to protect the grain from harm. The officiating priest at the Robigalia was the Flamen Quirinalis,[10] a fact which suggests a Sabine origin. The legend that it was founded by Numa [11] indicates the same idea.[12] Another festival which seems an echo of the Robigalia took place near a gate called Catularia. There reddish puppies were sacrificed to protect the crops.[13] Whether that sacrifice belonged to the Robigalia or to a festival which was a Roman double of it,[14] is for our purpose immaterial.

Another dog-cult was associated with two ancient and little known deities, the Lares Praestites. Ovid says that he sought to see their statues, but they had decayed with age.[15] He knew, however, that they were represented with a dog at their feet.[16] The Lares Praestites are thought to be portrayed on a coin of the Gens Caesia which shows two youths, each bearing a spear, and with a dog seated between them.[17]

Bust of Apollo seen from behind, holding thunderbolt in upraised right hand;
Rev. Lares Praestites seated facing, each holding staff in left hand;
between them, dog and above, bust of Vulcan with tongues over shoulder.

Plutarch adds the further fact that the Lares Praestites were clad in dog-skins.[18] The shrine of the Lares Praestites is by most authorities believed to have been on the Velia, on the same site as the Sacellum Larum which was erected by Augustus.[19] If that is true, the dog-cult of the Lares probably belonged to a later period than the ancient cults of the Cermalus, for the structures on the Velia are associated with the time when the Sabines made their way into Rome.[20] Plutarch puts the Lares Praestites in a class by themselves, asking why it is, that, of the Lares, those that are called by the individual name of *Praestites* are accompanied by a dog and wear dog-skins.[21] This question, together with the probable site of their shrine, suggests that the Lares Praestites were the Sabine Lares, as against the Lares Compitales, who were the protecting spirits of the Romans, and in whose cult the dog does not appear.[22] The prime function of the Lares is indicated by the prayer which the Arval Brothers, priests of the chthonic Dea Dia, offered to them, begging them to protect the people from all baleful forces.[23] Like Hecate, the Lares were worshipped at the crossroads,[24] but they also appeared as protecting deities in nearly all places.[23] The dog had, therefore, the same significance when associated with the Lares that he had with Hecate, for both were potent to protect from evil.

There are two other dog-cults of like character. The Umbrians offered a dog to their goddess Hontia.[25] Buecheler notes that the name Hontia is very similar to the name of the infernal regions and to certain words meaning destruction. He believes, accordingly, that the dog offered to Hontia was a purificatory sacrifice, designed to avert evil.[25] Another underworld goddess was Genita Mana, who is often regarded as identical with Mania.[26] Her realm, as is indicated by her name, was both birth and death.[27] To her a dog was sacrificed, with the prayer that none of the household might that year join the dead.[28] This sacrifice Plutarch makes parallel to the one offered by the Greeks to Hecate.[28] It was, therefore, designed to ward off the baleful powers of the under world.

Outside the cults with which the dog was especially associated, it often possessed for the Romans, as for the Greeks, a magic power. Puppies were considered so pure a meat, says Pliny, that they were used as expiatory sacrifices, and were served at the banquets given in honor of the gods.[29] The power of the dog to avert evil was utilized in a most practical way by the Roman farmers. Before undertaking any one of a variety of important tasks concerning the crops or the cattle, they took the precaution of sacrificing a dog. Also, by a sacrifice of this convenient animal, they might perform on festal days certain labors that would otherwise be forbidden.[30]

In all these cases of the dog as a sacred animal in Italy, we see that the Romans regarded it in the same light as did the Greeks, as a creature able to protect the people from evil, and especially potent to dispel the powers which were inimical to birth and growth. Therefore its use in the Lupercalia was wholly natural, that being a festival which sought to ward off evil and to set free the life-activities.

The instances of dog-sacrifice which have been found in Italy, occurred either in the immediate environs of Rome or in Umbria; but a series of coins which bear the figure of a dog seems to indicate that the dog was honored as a sacred animal throughout the southern half of Italy. A coin of Metapontum shows, back of a head of the city's mythical founder, a dog seated, with fore-paw raised.[31] The reverse pictures, as do many of the coins of Metapontum [32] an ear of grain. We remember that an ear of grain frequently occurred in conjunction with the dog on the coins of Segesta.[33] In the Apulian town of Larinum, a coin was issued representing a dog walking, with one foot raised; the reverse bears a head of Minerva.[34] A coin of Campania also shows a dog with fore-paw raised.[35] A dog with the same peculiarity of posture appears on a coin which is thought to come from Alba Fucentis. This coin portrays also an archaic wheel,[36] a symbol which was often used on Sicilian coins in conjunction with the dog.[37] A similar type comes from the town of Tuder, in southern Umbria.[38] Belonging to Hatria, a town of Picenum, is a coin which portrays the head of Silanus on one side, and a sleeping dog on the other.[39] A coin that is thought to have come from Etruria, shows the head of a youth, who was, perhaps, Hercules, and a dog.[40]

These coins, like the instances of dog-sacrifice in Italy, do not present the cult of one dog-shaped deity, but suggest, rather, a potent animal that was annexed by various gods. The dog-cults of Italy give no indication that they were a native development. There is no definite region from which they originated, nor is there any one deity to whom the dog was markedly sacrosanct. No contrast could be greater than between the faint and scattered fragments of the cult of the dog in Italy and the dominant figure of Hecate in Thrace.

If the cult of the dog was imported into Italy, it must have been at an early date, as it was associated with very ancient deities. Foreign rites were first brought to Rome from the Greek cities of Sicily and of Southern Italy.[41] We have seen that the dog-cult was strongly centered in Sicily, and that it was honored by the Mamertines when they occupied Messana.[42] Certain of the motives on the coins of Italy which were used in connection with the dog, as the sheaf of grain and the wheel, were also used in Sicily. The cult of the dog was also wide-spread in the cities of Southern Italy. The coins from bath Southern and Central Italy which show the dog with fore-paw raised, indicate, by this similarity of treatment, that there had been an exchange of ideas between those localities. The natural conclusion is that the worship of the dog, like so many early cults, was carried to Central Italy by the Greek traders who, as early as the time of the Tarquins, paid frequent visits to that region.[43]

If the cult of the dog among the Italians was a Greek importation, the dog-sacrifice cannot have been an original part of the Lupercalia, which antedated the arrival of the Greek cults. Though

Plutarch gives no hint of when the dog was first sacrificed in the Lupercalia, the complete lack of legends about it seems to indicate that it did not belong to the oldest stratum of the festival. In the Lupercalia, as well as in the Robigalia, the dog was sacrificed in conjunction with another victim. That may well indicate an, extension of the original ceremony, for outworn cults were often rejuvenated by the inclusion of new rites, or the sacrifice of a more unusual victim.[44] In Greece the sacrifice of a dog was at times severed from the worship of Hecate and used merely as a magic rite of purification.[45] In Italy the dog-sacrifice was devoted to purposes of magic.[46] Thus the sheep sacrificed at the Robigalia and the goat at the Lupercalia may well have had "new magic" given to them by the additional sacrifice of a dog.

We cannot be sure of the agency by which this new victim was added to the Lupercalia. It may have been brought in from the cities of Latium, just as was the cult of Heracles or of the Dioscuri. The fact, however, that the chief priest of the Sabines offered the dog to Robigus, and that the Sabines seem to have introduced the Lares Praestites to Rome, suggests the possibility that they were likewise responsible for the sacrifice of a dog at the Lupercalia. The character of the Sabines and the part which they played in the religion of the Romans gives added ground for this assumption.

The Sabines hold a place apart from ot her Italic tribes, for they universally adopted the Mediterranean custom of burying, instead of cremating, their dead. In the vast necropolis of Aufidena, not a single incineration-grave has been found.[47] This departure from the burial customs of their race proves that there had been some vital alteration in the Sabines. Furthermore, even the skulls found in these graves are dolicocephalic.[48] In religion the Sabines show a strong tendency toward chthonic cults.[49] For example, the Flamen Quirinalis performed the offering at the tomb of Acea Larentia and officiated at the Consualia, at which the altar of Consus, which was buried in the earth during the rest of the year, was uncovered.[50] The ancients considered the Sabines remarkable for their devotion to religion, as is shown by the popular derivation of *Sabini* from σέβομαι.[51] Also they ascribed to the Sabine kings, Numa and Titus Tatius, the majority of the important cults of Rome, thus expressing their belief that the Sabines had exercised a very great influence upon the development of religion in the Roman state.[52] Owing to this devout temperament, the Sabines would have been particularly ready to adopt the cult of the dog, for that, with its emphasis upon uncleanness and the need of purification, appealed to the most pious, as was shown when the Orphics made Hecate one of their chief gods.[53]

February, the month in which the Lupercalia was celebrated, was by legend connected with the Sabines. It was generally believed by the ancients that Numa, having divided the year into twelve months, instead of ten as heretofore, added the months of January and February.[54] The latter month derived its name from the *Jebrua,* the most solemn lustral media,[55] and was thus marked as the month of cleansing. Ovid says that when the year was only ten months in length, the Romans did not know the holy *februa.*[56] Though this statement need not be taken as literally true, it shows that Ovid believed that the Romans, were indifferent to the rite of purification, but that the Sabines valued it and were chiefly responsible for February being devoted to lustral ceremonies. Of all these cleansing rites, the Lupercalia had, by Varro's time, come to be the most important. Varro even went so far as to suggest that the whole month had derived its name from the Lupercalia, which he called "the day of purification."[57] It is reasonable to think of the Sabines as responsible, at least in part, for this emphasis upon the lustral side of the Lupercalia, since that festival could hardly have failed to be influenced by the dominant note which the Sabines seem to have given to the whole month of February. It was, moreover, not a new meaning that was thus added to the Lupercalia, but an intensifying and clarifying of its oldest significance, that of protecting men from evil. For, as the Mediterranean people developed in religious thought, they came to believe that the chief cause of evil was man's impurity, and hence strove to avert evil by removing impurity. Consequently the Lupercalia could best perform its ancient function if it freed the people from uncleanness.

The ritual acts of the Lupercalia, like those of all ceremonies of purgation, would tend to diminish in power.[58] We see this exemplified repeatedly in Rome's history. It would, therefore, have been fully in accord with the march of events that the Lupercalia, at some time of need, should likewise have failed the people, and that persons who were familiar with the efficacy of the sacrifice of a dog, should then have added that rite to the festival.

The Lupercalia started out as a ceremony of riddance. But the *riddance* of the infernal spirits is merely the savage man's way of putting it. Civilized man realizes that one must be *rid* of impurities that clog the life-power. Thus only could the gift of fertility, which was also sought by the Lupercalia, be assured. Among the Mediterranean people the most effective medium for this purpose was the sacrifice of a dog. This was a rite that was highly esteemed by the Sabines, who had adopted many beliefs of the Mediterranean race. The activity of the Sabines in reorganizing the religion of Rome and in developing the rites of purification, makes it easy to believe that they may have sought to fortify the Lupercalia, the oldest lustral ceremony of the city, by adding to it the most effective purificatory sacrifice that could be offered—a dog.

NOTES

1. Peter, in Roscher, iv, 826; Hild, in Daremberg-Saglio, iv, 1344.
2. Keller, *Die Antike Tierwelt*, i, 136, 140. 3. Plin., 8. 151.
4. Liebrecht, *Zur Volkskunde*, 23; Gruppe, 803-4.
5. Serv. ad Verg., *Georg.*, l. 151; Plin., *N. H.*, 18. 154, 161.
6. Gell., 5. 12. 14. Fowler *(R. F.,* 89) regards Robigus as an indigitation of Mars. This is merely another view of the same idea, for Mars was implored by Cato *(R.R.,* 141) to spare the crops from harm; and the mildew was the most dreaded form of injury.
7. The Robigalia is entered in the *Fasti* in large capitals, hence is one of the oldest festivals.
8. Var., *L. L.,* 6. 16; Paul. ex Fest., 267. Ovid *(Fast.,* 4. 939) offers in explanation of the dog-sacrifice the reason that it was to propitiate the dog-star, which was destructive to the crops. Dr. Fowler *(R. F.,* 90) has shown the falsity of this explanation. See also Hild, in Daremberg-Saglio, iv, 875.
9. See p.70 O.M.
10. Ov., *Fast.,* 4. 910.
11. Plin., *N. H.,* 18.285; Tertull., *de Spect.,* 5.
12. The objection may be raised that the Robigalia is often believed to have been held, not in the land of the Sabines, but on the Via Clodia, two miles beyond the Tiber (Fowler, *R. F.,* 89). This belief rests upon the identification of the Via Clodia with the Via Claudia, upon which, the Fasti state (C. *I. L.,* i, p. 392), the Robigalia was celebrated; but it is very hard to reconcile with Ovid's statement *(Fast.,* 4. 905) that he met the procession of the Robigalia when he was going from Nomentum to Rome. If Mommsen's explanation (C. *I. L.,* i, p. 392), that Ovid was going to his gardens which lay near the Via Clodia, is to be accepted, one must believe that Ovid described his route in a very ambiguous fashion. On the other hand, if Ovid's words are taken at face value, they would mean that the Lucus Robiginis was in the Sabine country between Rome and Nomentum. Since this territory had been held

by the Claudian tribe from prehistoric times (Verg., *Aen,*. 706-12; Liv., 2. 16. 5; Suet., *Tib.*, I; Pinza, *Monumenti primitivi di Roma e del Lazio antico,* 221), it would have been very natural that a road passing through it should be known as the Via Claudia. This explanation also obviates the difficulty arising from the discrepancy of the names Via Claudia, mentioned in the Fasti, and Via Clodia; for the latter name never appears in inscriptions or itineraries in any other form.

13. Fest., 285; Paul. ex Fest., 45.
14. This is the view of Mommsen (C. *I. L.*, i, 392) and of Fowler (*R. F.*,90).
15. *Fast.*, 5. 143.
16. *Fast.*, 5. 137.
17. Babelon, i, 281; Jordan, *De larum imaginibus,* 329.
18, *Q. R.*, 51. Some scholars believe that a dog was also sacrificed to the Lares Praestites (Fowler, *R. F.,* 101; Roscher, i, 1612).
19. Jordan, *Lar. im.*, 326-9; Becker, *De Romae veteris muris atqueportis,* 12; Wissowa, *R. K.,* 171.
20. Both Numa and Ancus Martius are said to have dwelt on the Velia (Solin., 21, 23). Numa was said to have built the Regia (Ov., *Trist.*, 3. I. 30) and the temple of Vesta (Dionys., 2. 65,66).
21. *Q. R.*, 51.
22. Fowler, R. F.,101.
23. Henzen, *Acta Fratrum Arvalium,* 145.
24. Ov., *Fast.*, 5. 140; Macr., 1. 7.35.
25. Buecheler, *Umbrica,*128.
26. Muller, *Etrusker,* ii, 105 n. 78b.
27. Roscher, i,1612.
28. Plut., *Q. R.*, 52; Plin., *N. H.*, 29. 58,
29. *N. H.*, 29. 58.
30. Colum., 2. 22.
31. *Hunterian Collection,* 9r.24.
32. *Hunterian Collection,*91.
33. See p.70 O.M.
34. Babelon, i,29.
35. *Hunterian Collection,* 52. 33, Pl. iv .8.
36. *Hunterian Collection,* 11. I.
37. See p.70 O.M.
38. Head, 22; *Hunterian Collection,*5.
39. Head, 23; *Hunterian Collection,*7.
40. *Hunterian Collection,*18.
41. Fowler, *R. F.,*197.
42. See p.70 O.M.
43. Carter, *The Religious Life of Ancient Rome,* 39; Pais, *Anc. It.*. 289; Fowler, *R. F.,* 121; Schwegler, i, 679.
44. Fowler, *R. E.,*287.
45. See p.68 O.M.

46. See p.76 O.M.

47. Modestov, 254.

48. Modestov, 255.

49. Piganiol, 30, 132, *et passim.*

50. Tertull., *de Spect.*, 8; Ge ll., 7. 7. 7.

51. Var. ap. Fest., 343; Schwegler, i, 244.

52. Wissowa, *R. K.*, 430; Fowler, *R. E.*, 108; Schwegler, i, 248;Marquardt, iii, 27-31.

53. See page 68 O.M.

54. Var., *L. L.*, 6. 34; Liv. 1. 19. 6; Ov., *Fast.*, 3. 152; Plut., *Num.*, 19; Solin., I. 37; Cens., 20. 2, 4, 5; Macr., 7. 13. 2-5. The following scholars are inclined to believe that the organization of the calendar was due to the Sabines: Huschke. *Das alte römische Jahr und seine Tage*, 8, 26; Wissowa, *R. K.*, 430; Marquardt, iii, 284; Fowler, *R. E.*, 108. The difficulties involved in the idea of a ten-month year (Fowler, *R. F.*, 2) cannot be considered here, but the names January and February show by their formation that they were later than the names of the other months (Schulze, *Zur Geschichte lateinischen Eigennamen*, 487).

55. Var. ap. Non., p. 114. 17; Censor., 22. 14; Ov., *Fast.*, 2. 19; Plut., *Q. R.*, 19; id. *Num.*, 19; Lyd., *de Mens.*, 4. 25. From these *februa* was fashioned the god Februus, an infernal deity, the double of Pluto (Serv. ad Verg., *Georg.*, I. I. 43; Isid., *Orig.*, 5. 33. 4; Macr., I. 13. 3; Gelas. *adv. Androm.*, 3). He was named by Lydus *(de Mens.*, 4. 25) the god of the Lupercalia. He was, however, evidently a late abstraction, as his name does not occur before the fourth century.

56. *Fast.*, 5. 423.

57. *L. L.*, 6. 34.

58. Diels, 83.

CHAPTER IX

The Blood-Ceremony of The Lupercalia

THERE REMAINS TO be considered the curious rite of the Lupercalia in which a sword was dipped into the blood of the sacrifice and pressed upon the foreheads of two young men. The blood was then washed away with wool moistened in milk. After that the youths mustlaugh.[1] This ceremony has provoked wide speculation because it is utterly different from the usual cult-practices of the Romans. To gain an understanding of the use and significance of these media, we must turn to the ritualistic acts of Greece.

Of the use of blood in primitive religions we have countless instances. The almost unvarying idea of uncivilized man is that blood is not merely essential to life, but the very life itself.[2] Consequently in sacrifices offered to earth-gods to stir their life-giving power, the blood of the victim is often poured upon the ground. By a transference of idea, since the sacrificial animal has within it the essence of the deity, its blood is regarded as the supreme embodiment of the god's mystic potency.[3] Man may partake of this divine power by various means: he may drink the blood, or he may have it applied to him externally, as was done in the Lupercalia. Thus he comes into contact with the life-force and is purified.[4] For this reason the blood of the sacrificial victim was used to cleanse men from murder and from madness.[5] In ceremonies of lustration, sprinkling with blood was the surest of all cleansing media.[6] It seems to have been employed as one of the lustral ceremonies of the Eleusinian Mysteries.[7] In the rite of the Taurobolium the worshipper, in a pit beneath the sacrificial animal, won purity by allowing the sacred blood to flow upon him until he was literally covered.[8] This ceremony, which was probably of great antiquity in Asia,[9] came to be practised in the Cybele-Attis cult as one of its most important features.[10] In Italy the Taurobolium was ardently observed during several centuries of the Empire.[11] The Orphics, who specialized in lustral media,[12] received into their religion the god Attis together with his bloody rite.[13] The Orphics put themselves into contact with the divine power in another ceremony, the Omophagia, in which they imbibed the sacrificial blood, along with the raw flesh, of the newly slain animal.[14]

In these instances of the use of blood in Greek ritual, it was either an offering to the earth-mother, that she might recreate into new life this life-force which was restored to her, or it was a means by which man, coming into direct contact with the essence of deity, might be freed from all the forces of evil. Freedom from evil was likewise the purpose of the Lupercalia, hence the use of blood in that festival may reasonably be regarded as parallel to that of the Greek ceremonies. The rite of blood-sprinkling, belonging as it did to the worship of chthonic deities, and appearing most markedly in the cult of Attis and in the ritual of the Orphics, may be accepted as characteristically Mediterranean.

In the chthonic cults of Italy, as in Greece, the blood of the sacrifice was frequently poured upon the earth. Thus it was offered to the Manes [16] and to Terminus.[16] In the quaint rite that occurred on the Ides of October, a horse was slain, his tail was suspended in the Regia and the blood allowed to drip upon the hearth. The blood was preserved, it seems, by the Vestal Virgins, and later, mixed with the ashes of unborn calves, was sprinkled upon the fires through which the people leaped in the Parilia.[17] Here blood is used in a mystic rite whose purpose is interpreted as the same as that of the Lupercalia—lustration and fertility.[18] But in the details of the ritual the two festivals offer no likeness such as we discovered in the Pelasgian ceremonies.

The sword by which the blood was placed upon the youths' heads should probably be classed with other weapons, such as the double axe and the figure-eight shield of Crete, which were holy objects in Mediterranean ritual.[19] The significance of the sacrificial sword in the Taurobolium is shown by its constant representation upon the Taurobolic altars.[20] The regular association of the sickle with Chronus suggests its sanctity in his cult.[21] In Italy the lance of Juno Quiritis and of Quirinus, and the lance and the *ancilia* of Mars were especially venerated.[22]

The blood smeared upon the foreheads of the young men was wiped off by a bit of wool dipped in milk. In the same way in Greek rites the sacrificial blood which had been sprinkled upon a man was removed by various cleansing media. "The blood was too holy to be left in permanent contact with a man who was presently to return to common life."[23] The Orphics frequently smeared earth upon the devotees as a means of cleansing, and removed it by a ceremonial *wiping off.*[24] So important in ceremonies of purification was this bedaubing with clay and its removal that the words περιμάττειν and ἀπομάττειν became standing expressions for mystic cleansing.[26] Of this ceremonial *wiping off* the Lupercalia affords the only example in Roman cults.

From the sanctity which the skin of a sacrificial animal possessed, it is natural that wool should have been of significant and constant use in the religion of both Greeks and Romans. The binding of the priest's forehead with woolen fillets before he sacrificed, was a symbol that he was possessed by the deity.[26] Naturally, therefore, wool was potent for purification. Ovid, in his list of the materials that have cleansing power, mentions wool first of all.[27] Wool was included among the offerings of first fruits and natural products which were placed in the *kernos* and carried as holy objects in the Mysteries of Eleusis.[28]

Milk, used in the Lupercalia to moisten the wool, was employed among both Greeks and Romans in the earliest times as a libation to chthonic deities. But of its mystic use in the Lupercalia, native Roman religion affords us no other instance. That meaning can be found only in the religion of the Orphics. The use of milk in the Orphic mysteries is indicated by certain gold tablets which are very important sources of knowledge of the Orphic cults. These tablets were placed close by the dead person and contained directions for his conduct in the lower world: formulas that he was to repeat, or statements of ritual that he had performed. They constituted for the dead man his card of admission to the realm of the blest.[29]

The close similarity of phrasing in the tablets indicates that they echo some important ritualistic poem of the Orphics.[30] Two tablets contain the words, *"Thou shalt be god instead of mortal. A kid, I have fallen into milk".*[31] These words, like the other formulas, must describe some symbolic act which the initiate has performed. The promise, "Thou shalt be god instead of mortal" suggests that the following words, "A kid, I have fallen into milk," express in mystic fashion the Orphic's attainment of the highest bliss. The meaning of *a kid* in this formula has been explained by Dr. Dieterich, who notes that $E\rho\iota\phi\iota\sigma s$ was a title of Dionysus which was used by the Dorians of the Peloponnesus and of Southern Italy, being especially favored at Metapontum, near which these tablets were found.[32] Thus in this region Dionysus was known as "The Kid," just as he was called "The Bull" in Crete. Consequently, when the Orphic calls himself *a kid* he seems to identify himself with the Kid Dionysus.[33] But "The Kid" is an infant god, and so must be nourished upon milk.[34] By the use of milk, therefore, the initiates further symbolized their union with the god.[35] The expression, "I have fallen," has been taken to indicate an actual bath in milk,[36] or a vigorous substitute for the words, "I have found," the worshipper's complete union with the deity being probably symbolized by his drinking milk or being sprinkled with milk.[37] In either case, the words, "A kid, I have fallen into milk" seem to indicate that the initiate has been mystically reborn and transformed into a god.[37] The same idea appears in the cult of Cybele. In the sacred drama, after Attis has died and has been restored to life, the worshippers end their mourning fast by partaking of milk. In doing so they seem to be in divine communion with the youthful god, who has just entered life anew.[38]

The laughter of the youths, which formed the final act of the blood-ceremony, finds no parallel in Roman cult, and very little in Greek. It has been explained (a) as the indication by the lads of their readiness to be sacrificed,[39] (b) as the sign that, after their ritualistic slaughter, they were restored to life,[40] and (c) as the symbol of their entranc upon a new life of purity.[41] If we are correct in our belief that a human being was not the original victim at the Lupercalia, neither of the first two explanations of the laugh can be accepted. On the other hand, the third view, that it was the expression of joy over being cleansed and so restored to new life, is in complete harmony with the symbolism of the purifying blood and the milk. If so, it corresponds to the joyous words uttered by the Orphic after he had been purified by the smearing on and the wiping off of mud, "Bad have I fled, better have I found.[42] The cult of Attis, in which the blood and the milk had a part so similar to their use in the Lupercalia, offers another parallel. After the communicants had ended their mourning for Attis and had received milk as the sign of their admission to a new life, they celebrated the festival called Ἱλαρεία.[43] The uncontrolled expression of joy which characterized that festival may be likened to the laughter that concluded the Lupercalia.

As we sum up the significance of this strange part of the Luper calia, we see that, almost without exception, the elements belong characteristically to Pelasgian religion. Sprinkling with blood as a means of purification or of communion with the deity, a ceremonial *wiping off* as a sign that old things are done away, and a sprinkling with milk symbolizing a new life of purity and of kinship with divinity, were, to many Greeks, ritual acts that called forth profound reverence. Of such rites the cults indigenous to Italy give us not a single instance except the Lupercalia. That suggests the possibility that this bit of ritual was borrowed, as were so many elements of the Roman religion, from the Greeks.[44]

If such was the case, the Orphics probably introduced these ceremonies; for only in their rites and in those of Attis, whom they took as their own god, were these acts significant. Was there any medium by which the influence of the Orphics could have become so pronounced in Rome as to account for a graft of their ritual upon this ancient Roman festival?

The Cumaean Sibyl immediately comes to the mind of one who seeks to explain the presence of a foreign cult in Rome. From very early days she had accustomed the Romans to receive Greek deities or to add Greek ceremonials to the nativerites.[45] Under her guidance one chthonic god after another, Demeter, Dionysus, Proserpina, Hennes, Poseidon, Dis, and Aesculapius, came to Rome. The ancient Roman cult of Saturn was Hellenized by the addition of a *lectisternium* and other features of Greek ritual. The ceremonials directed by the Sibyl were of a mystic or a spectacular type, appealing to the same emotions of awe or of religious enthusiasm as the ritual acts of the Orphics. The influence of the Sibyl was most marked during the war with Hannibal,[46] when the people seemed no longer able to secure help from their native gods, and so appealed repeatedly to the Sibyl. After Trasimene, a spectacular *lectisternium* was held: six pairs of gods, Greek and Roman being taken without distinction, were placed on couches to receive offerings. Dr. Warde

Fowler declares that this event marks the turning-point in Roman religion: "the dividing line between *di indigetes* and *di novensiles* now vanishes forever."[47] From now on, Greek ritual was employed alike for Greek and for Roman deities. After the disaster of Cannae many foreign rites were introduced. The people even resorted to a religious act utterly abhorrent to Romans:[48] two Gauls and two Greeks were buried alive in the Forum Boarium. Finally the Romans brought to their city, with all pomp, the statue of the Magna Mater of Pessinus. During the same year Dionysus was received in Rome. These last arrivals were not accorded the treatment given to other foreign gods: they were not kept outside the Pomoerium, but were given temples on the Palatine, just above the ancient cult-center on the Cermalus, hence close by the Lupercal. Owing to this proximity, these two powerful deities had an excellent opportunity to influence the cult of Lupercus. The Phrygian Cybele, though she was not usually included among the variant names of the Orphic deity, was the same in essence and was honored by the same mystic and orgiastic rites; while the worship of Dionysus might be called the kernel of Orphic religion.[49]

For the direct influence of Orphism upon Rome, we must turn to the cities of Southern Italy, with which Rome, even under the Etruscans, had active trade relations.[50] In the wake of the traders various Greek gods, as, for example, Heracles and the Dioscuri, made their way into Rome.[51] Damia, the earth-goddess of Tarentum, was identified with Bona Dea, and imposed certain features of her ritual upon the native cult.[52] The foisting of Greek rites upon so ancient a goddess as Bona Dea is especially significant. In these Greek cities of Southern Italy, Orphism was honored more than in any other region. The teachings of Orpheus were accepted as the basic principles of the school of Pythagoras, which was established at Velia, and which was influential throughout the neighboring cities.[53] Some of the Orphic tablets mentioned above were unearthed at Sybaris.[54] At Tarentum both the ritual of Pythagoras and the mysteries of Dionysus were especially cultivated.[55] With these particular cities, Velia, Tarentum, and Sybaris, Rome had especially active communication from the earliest times.[56] During the Samnite Wars the Romans came to know the Pythagoreans in their own home. Appius Claudius Caecus is said to have embraced their faith,[57] and even the hard headed elder Cato was interested in listening to their theories.[58] The vogue which this philosophy gained in Rome is evidenced by the persistent tradition that Numa was a Pythagorean.[59]

By 181 B.C. Pythagoreanism was strong enough in Rome to attempt a daring fraud. On Mount Janiculum was dug up a coffin bearing an inscription which declared that it contained the body of Numa. Within it were found, not a skeleton, but books on Pythagorean philosophy which purported to be the writings of Numa.[60] The purpose must have been to win state support for mysticism under the prestige of Numa's name. The hope that such an attempt could succeed argues a rather wide-spread acceptance in Rome of Pythagorean philosophy. But the ruse was doomed to failure: the Senate immediately denounced these Orphic books as a fraud, and ordered that they be burned in the Comitium.[60] A companion picture to this occurrence is furnished by an outbreak five years earlier, when a large, part of the populace turned with the utmost abandon to the orgies of Dionysus. Meetings were held at night, and the wild frenzy which prevailed in Thrace or on Mount Cithaeron was rampant in Rome. In this case, too, the Senate took firm measures. This strange religion was denounced as a *coniuratio,* and the celebrants punished as conspirators against the state. Yet the Senate provided a safety valve for their religious fervor. Under carefully stipulated conditions, those who felt that they could not conscientiously give up the new religion, were allowed to continueit.[61] These two events coming so close together, show very clearly the following which the religious ecstasy and the mystic ritual acts of the Orphics had won in Rome. So threatening were the proportions of this new cult that the Senate did, not dare follow its usual practice of religious tolerance; and yet infection so intense and so widespread must not be deprived of an outlet, lest the evil break forth still more violently. A judicious state control was, therefore the solution.[62]

This survey of the influence of the Cumaean Sibyl and of Orphism upon Rome shows that a transfer of Orphic rites to an ancient Roman ceremony like the Lupercalia was inherently possible. For centuries the Romans were bringing in one after another of the primitive chthonic deities of Greece, were identifying various Italian gods with Greek gods, and altering the established national ritual to suit Greek practices. At any time during this period the partial Hellenizing of the Lupercalia would have been in harmony with the spirit of the times. Such a change could have occurred most easily, however, during the Hannibalic war or the two decades immediately following, when the people, having received into their city Cybele and Dionysus, were deeply stirred by the orgies of Dionysus and by the beliefs of the Pytagoreans. During that period the insertion of certain Orphic rites into the Lupercalia would have been only one event of numberless such. Moreover, the Lupercalia, with its emphasis upon purification, would have been an especially natural ceremony to receive an Orphic graft; for purification was above all else the quest of the Orphics, and they were expert in the media by which to attain it.

Assuming that the blood-rite of the Lupercalia may have been of Orphic origin, we observe that no one ceremony was taken over bodily by the Romans, but that this part of the Lupercalia must have been, rather, a psychological product. The people's state of mind during the war with Hannibal is clearly indicated by the numerous portents which were announced. Early in the war came an omen suggesting that Mars, the later incarnation of the old wolf-deity, had forsaken his people: a wolf came and snatched a guard's sword from its sheath and carried it off.[63] A little later the statues of the wolf which were in Rome, sweated.[64] Such omens as these may easily have caused the people to consider with concern the ceremony at the wolf's cave, and to wonder if that, like so many others, had lost its power to protect them. Frequently in the first alarm of Hannibal's arrival in Italy, blood appeared among the omens. Two shields exuded drops of blood; the springs at Caere and the fount of Hercules were stained with blood; at Arretium the reapers found themselves harvesting bloody heads of grain; and after the battle of Cannae blood flowed in the river beside Amiternum.[65] These omens of blood are a wholly natural phenomenon during the carnage of war; but it would be equally natural that rites which employed blood as a means of purification should appeal to the people. In magic and in religious rites akin to magic, the homeopathic principle that like cures, like is always potent. Assuming that the insertion of the blood-rite in to the Lupercalia could most easily have occurred during the emotional turmoil caused by the Hannibalic war, we may perhaps define the probable date still more closely. The first few years of the war offer the least probability. Livy tells explicitly the alarming prodigies that occurred at that time, and the strange expedients adopted to annul them. Had the ceremony of the Lupercalia been altered then, we should certainly expect it to be mentioned along with the other innovations. But as the war goes on, Livy gives much less detail. Probably his artistic sense rebelled at painting the same picture too often. After the battle of Cannae, he contents himself with saying that various prodigies occurred, and that certain unusual ceremonies were perfonned.[66] Three years later, when there was another outburst of omens, he passes on with the mere statement, "Due measures were taken by decree of the pontiffs."[67] As the war dragged on, "Such religious fervor," Livy says, "assailed the state, *and in large part of foreign origin at that,* that it seemed as if either men or gods must have completely changed." Not only within private houses was the Roman ritual broken down, but even in the Forum and in the Capitol were disorderly throngs of women who, neither in their prayers nor in their sacrifices, followed the ritual of their ancestors.[68] Following this, came the command of the Senate that no foreign rites be performed at any national shrine.[69] This order, on the one hand, shows, that alien ritual acts had invaded the established state ceremonials of the Romans; but, on the other hand, makes it improbable that the blood-rite of the Lupercalia, if added to the ceremony at this time, would have continued. Therefore the years following this occurrence offer a more reasonable time for such a change. The Dionysia of 186 B.C. and the discovery of the Pythagorean Books in 181 certainly cannot have been isolated outbreaks. Had Livy chosen to give us in detail the changes in religious ritual, which occurred during the latter part of the period of the foreign wars, he might have resolved for us many a knotty problem. As it is, we have to admit that after the first two years of the war with Hannibal there occurred many alterations in religious belief and form of which we know nothing. Among these innovations which Livy passes over in silence, might easily have been an addition of Orphic rites to the Lupercalia.

It is interesting that Plutarch, the only author to mention the blood-ritual, connects its origin with a war. But, just as the temple of Jupiter Stator, which was actually built in 294 B.C., was referred to Romulus, so this part of the Lupercalia was said to be a memorial of the struggle of Romulus with Amulius, "the blood symbolizing the bloodshed and terror of that time." [70]

A scrap of evidence suggests that the blood-ceremony was not a part of the original rites of the Lupercalia. Plutarch, when speaking of those upon whom the blood-rite was performed, always uses the word boys, μειράκια. This seems an impossible term to apply to the Luperci. Mark Antony was consul when he acted as a Lupercus.[71] The μειράκια, therefore, must have been other than the priests of Lupercus. Presumably they were admitted into the ceremony for the express purpose of this blood-ritual. But this would give a clear indication that the blood-rite was not an original part of the festival.

If it had been, the Luperci would have been the natural persons for the central figures, not two striplings. Livy says that the missionaries of Dionysus in Rome sought especially to win the young to their mysteries, and that many youths of high rank became enthusiastic devotees.[72] The same wave of emotion may have introduced the boys and their mystic rites into the Lupercalia.

If such was the case, the events that immediately followed explain why Plutarch is the only one who mentioned this strange part of the festival. The prompt measures taken to combat the Dionysia and the relentless destruction of the Pythagorean books, show that the Roman authorities were resolved to rescue their state religion from these emotional beliefs that were threatening to engulf it. The same purpose is manifest in the treatment of the cult of Cybele: native Romans were forbidden to join her priesthood, and the priests were restricted, except on certain days of the year, to their own precincts.[73] It was not until the time of Claudius that the Magna Mater was restored to full honor.[74] In view of this state policy, we can well understand that Orphic rites, if introduced into the Lupercalia, would soon have been thrust into the background. In accord with this policy of supression, priests and the compilers of the Fasti would naturally have avoided making any record of the addition of these foreign rites to the Lupercalia. Thus the silence upon that subject of all writers except Plutarch would be reasonably accounted for. Almost certainly Ovid knew nothing of this ceremony. It was the Greek poet Butas, who would naturally have been interested in this rite of his own people, who seems to have been Plutarch's authority. Plutarch is, likewise, the only one to comment upon the sacrifice of the dog, a rite more characteristically Greek than Roman.

The trifling evidence which we have to apply to this problem is, at least, not against the theory that the blood-rite may have been introduced into the Lupercalia during the second Punic War or the years immediately following. This theory is wholly in accord with reason. We have, as it were, two sides of an equation, and it is tempting to place between them the sign of equality: on the one side, there is in the Lupercalia an incongruous bit of ceremonial which has no unity with the other cult-acts of the festival, and which finds no parallel in the ritualistic practices of the Romans, but which is markedly like many Greek rites, especially those of the Orphics; on the other hand, there is the reception in Rome of a stream of Greek deities and cults, the process being intensified by the strain of a great war, when the people repeatedly sought help from just such mystic rites as this of the Lupercalia. The old ceremonial, devised to rid man of all that would obstruct the activity of deific power, would then have been spiritualized by the Orphic's assurance of perfect cleansing and of communion, even of kinship, with divinity.

NOTES
1. Plut., *Rom.*, 21.
2. Tylor, ii; 38r.
3. Gruppe, 891.
4. Stengel, *Die Griechischen Kultusaltertümer*, 139-42.
5. Aesch., *Eum.*, 283; Apoll. Rhod., 4. 477-9, 704.
6. Stengel, *Opferbräuche der Griechen*, 30; Diels, *Sibyllinische Blatter*,73.
7. Farnell, iii,168.
8. Prudent., *Peristeph.*, 10.1011-50.
9. Cumont, *The Mysteries ofMithra*,.180.
10. Decharrne, in Daremberg-Saglio, i, 1686.

11. Espérandieu, in Daremberg-Saglio, v, 50.

12. Stengel; *Kultusalt.,* 150.

13. Farnell, iii, 302.

14. Harrison, 481-9; Monceaux, in Daremberg-Saglio, iv, 253.

15. Verg., *Aen.,* 3. 63-7.

16. Ov., *Fast.,* 2. 655.

17. Fest., 178; Ov., *Fast.,* 4. 731-4; Prop., 4. l. 18.

18. Fowler, *R. F.,*247.

19. Mackenzie, *Crete,* 310-2. See also above, page 6.

20. Espérandieu, in Daremberg-Saglio, v, 48, 49.

21. Lippert, ii, 498.

22. Preller, i, 339.

23. Smith, *Semites,* 351; see also Schoemann, *Griechische Altertümer,* ii, 13.

24. Nonnus Dionys., 27. 228; Poll., *Onomast.,* 8. 65; 7. 188; Harpocrat., ἀτομάττων.

25. Demosth., *de Cor.,* 259; Ammonius, περιμάξαι; Lucian, *Necy.,*7.

26. Lippert, ii, 537; Diets, 122.

27. *Fast.,* 2.19-28.

28. Athen., II. 56. p. 478 d; Harrison, 159-60.

29. Kaibel, *C. I. G. I. S.,* 481 a, b, c. For the discussion of these tablets, see Dieterich, *Hym. orph.,* 30-7; id., *Nekyia,* 84-95; Harrison, 573-99.

30. Reinach, *Une formule orphique,* in *Rev. Arch.,* vol. xxxix, 204.

31. Kaibel, *C. I. G. I. S.,* 642, 481 a. See also Harrison, 584, 586.

32. *Hym. orph.,* 36. See also Hesych., Ἐρίφιος.

33. Reinach, *Rev. Arch.* vol. xxxix, 207; id. *Cultes,* ii. 128; Cook, *Zeus,* 674-5.

34. Dieterich, *Eine Mithrasliturgie,* 171. Milk was one of the gifts which streamed from the earth for the worshippers of Dionysus (Eur. *Bacch.,* 142, 708, *etal.).*

35. Reinach, *Cultes,* ii, 128.

36. Cook, *Zeus,*675-7.

37. Reinach, *Cultes,* ii, 129-32; id. *Rev. Arch.,* vol. xxxix, 206; Harrison, 594-7.

38. Farnell, iii., 301. This corresponds to the usage of the early Christians, by which milk was offered to the new communicants as the sign of new birth (Usener, *Milch und Honig, Rhein. Mus.,* vol. vii, 183).

39. Lippert, ii, 564.

40. Mannhardt, *Myth. Forsch.,* 98.

41. Deubner, *Arch. Rel.,* vol. xiii, 502.

42. Demos., *de Cor.* 313.

43. Farnell, iii,301.

44. Dr. Deubner *(Arch. Rel.,* vol. xiii, 506-8) believes that the blood-ritual was borrowed from the Greeks, and that it signified purification and new birth. He holds, however, that it, and also the dog-sacrifice, was added to the Lupercalia under the influence of Augustus. In view of Augustus's rationalistic temperament and of his desire to restore the ancient cults of Rome , it is hard to accept this view.

45. For the earlier influence exerted by the Cumaean Sibyl upon the religionof Rome, see Wissowa, *R. K.,* 50-2; Fowler, *R. E.,* 255-66; Carter, *Rel. Rome,* 40-5.

46. For a survey of the changes effected in Roman religion durign this period, see Fowler, *R. E.*, 314-31; Wissowa, *R. K.*, 58-64; Carter, *Religion of Numa*, 104-15.
47. *R. E.*, 319.
48. Liv., 22. 57. 6.
49. Harrison, 455.50. Seep. 81 n. 43.
51. Wissowa, *R. K.*, 268- 73.
52. Fowler, *R. F.*, 105.
53. Cic., *Tusc.*, I. 38; Liv., I. 18. 2.
54. See p.85 O.M.
55. Dieterich, *Hym. orph.*, 39.
56. Schwegler, i, 683; Pais , *Anc. It.*, 303-44.
57. Cic., *Tusc.*, 4. 2. 4.
58. Cic., *Cat. M.;* 78.
59. Liv., I. 18. 2.
60. Liv., 40. 29; Plin., *N. H.*, 13. 84-6.
61. Liv., 39. 8-16.
62. Fowler, *R. E.*, 344-9
63. Liv., 21. 62. 4.
64. Liv., 22. 1. 12.
65. Liv., 22. I. 9, rn; 22. 36. 7; 24. 44. 8.
66. Liv., 22. 57. 2, 6.
67. Liv., 24. 44. 9,
68. Liv., 25. 1. 6-8.
69. Liv., *25.* 1.
70. Plut., *Rom.*, 21.
71. Suet., *Jul.*, 79.
72. See note 61. See also Fowler, *R. E.*,347.
73. Dionys., 2. 79.
74. Cumont, *The Oriental Religions in Roman Paganism, 55,*

CHAPTER X

Resume

MORE THAN A thousand years before the Christian era, we may imagine the hills upon the Tiber occupied by scattered clans of Ligurians. From their remote ancestors they had inherited a religion that was mainly of fear, and that sought to propitiate the invisible forces that seemed lurking to do harm. To the people of Italy the wolf was a constant object of terror, and so it had very early come to typify this destructive power. Accordingly the tribes dwelling near the Palatine came to the Lupercal and tried to propitiate the wolf-deity that dwelt there. They offered a goat from their herds, then fled with all speed from the scene of the slaughter of a sacred animal. Afterward, having expiated their guilt, they returned to the cave, to partake in sacramental fashion of the victim. In this, its earliest stage, the Lupercalia was an apotropaic rite whose purpose was protection against evil.

When the *terramara* folk settled upon the Palatine, they found the cult at the wolf-cave too long established and too deeply venerated to be eradicated or disregarded. Therefore they incorporated it into their religion, and had their own priests share in the ritual.

Yet the part assigned to the new-comers was shadowy; the Ligurian priests performed all the significant rites. In time the practical Romans observed that the goat-sacrifice which they offered at the Lupercal lacked the vigor possessed by it in the neighboring cults of Juno Caprotina and Juno Lucina, in which blows from the victim's hide assured to the worshippers the entrance of the god's life-giving power. So they proceeded to reinforce the rite of Lupercus with these cult-acts of Juno. Thus the Lupercalia had a new purpose added to the old one: it now served to assure the people of fertility.

After the cult of the dog had appeared in Italy, a dog-sacrifice was regarded as an especially potent means of purification. It was, accordingly, adopted by the Sabines, an intensely devout people, who regarded man's impurity as the root of all disaster. It is not hard to believe that, when the Sabines took under their care some of the oldest chthonic cults of Rome, and devoted the month of February wholly to cleansing rites, they sought to add potency to the Lupercalia, which occurred in the middle of this lustral period, by including in its rites the sacrifice of a dog. According to the interpretation of the Sabines, the Lupercalia could best perform its old purpose of protection and fertility by assuring the people of purification.

As directed by the Roman priesthood, Rome's religion tended to become stereotyped and formalistic. At a time of peril it could offer little of support or of comfort. Consequently the dark days of the war with Hannibal witnessed the reception in Rome of an unbroken succession of chthonic gods and of their orgiastic rites. The outworn festivals of the native gods, who no longer helped the people, were revivified by the addition of Greek ceremonies. Such a time affords a natural setting for the introduction into the Lupercalia of acts which resemble nothing except the rites of the Orphics. These Orphic ceremonies possessed a power of lustration so strong that they assured to the celebrant an entrance into a new state, where he was one with the gods. Therefore if the effete ceremonial of the Lupercalia was reinforced by the Orphic sprinkling with blood for perfect cleansing, and the mystic use of milk in token of new life, it was a logical culmination of a festival that sought to protect the people from harm by making them pure.

In the development of the Lupercalia, the old was not replaced by the new so much as reinterpreted by it. Protection against evil involved, on its positive side, the assurance of productivity. For that, cleanness of the worshipper was essential, hence the ceremony became dominantly lustral. According to later theology, when man was fully cleansed, he became akin to the gods. Having thus been reinforced by successive new ideas, this oldest of Rome's festivals was the last to succumb to Christianity. Even when Pope Gelasius abrogated it, he softened his act by establishing on the same day a festival celebrating the purification of the Virgin.[1] Thus transformed, the Lupercalia, in its essential meaning, continued to live on.

NOTE
1. Baronius, *Annales Ecclesiastici,* 8. 60 fol.

BIBLIOGRAPHY

(This list is not a complete bibliography. It includes simply the volumes that have been quoted or referred to in this dissertation.)

• ADAM, JAMES. The Religious Teachers of Greece. Edinburgh, 1909.
• D'ARBOIS DE JUBAINVILLE, HENRY. Les premiers habitants de l'Europe
  d'après les écrivains de l'antiquité et les travaux des linguistes. 2 vol-
  umes. Paris, 1889-94.
• AUST, EMIL. Die Religion der Römer. Münster, 1899.
• BABELON, ERNEST, Monnaies de la république romaine. 2 volumes.
  Paris, 1885-6.
• BECKER, WILHELM A. De Romae veteris muris atque portis. Leipzig,
  1842.
• BEDDOE, JOHN, The Anthropological History of Europe. Paisley, 1912.
• BELOCH, JULIUS. Griechische Geschichte. 2 volumes. Strassburg, 1912-14.
• BRITISH MUSEUM. Coins of Thrace. See Poole, R. S.
• BUECHELER, FRANZ. Umbrica. Bonn, 1883.
• BURROWS, RONALD M. The Discoveries in Crete London, 1908.
• CAMPBELL, LEWIS. Religion in Greek Literature. London, New York, and
  Bombay, 1898.
• CARTER, JESSE. The Religion of Numa. London and New York, 1906. (Numa)
  – The Religious Life of Ancient Rome. Boston and NewYork, 1911. (Rel.
  Rome)
• CHADWICK, HECTOR MUNRO. The Heroic Age. Cambridge, 1912.
• COOK, ARTHUR B. Animal Worship in the Mycenaean Age. Journal of
  Hellenic Studies, vol. xiv, 1894.
  – Zeus, a Study in Ancient Religion, vol. i. Cambridge, 1914.
• COTTERILL, H. B. Ancient Greece, New York, 1913.
• CUMONT, FRANZ. The Mysteries of Mithra (translated from the second
  revised edition of the French by T. J . McCormack). Chicago, 1910.
  – The Oriental Religions in Roman Paganism (authorized translation).
  Chicago, 1911.
• DAREMBERG, C., et SAGLIO, E. Dictionnaire des antiquités grecques et
  romaines. 5 volumes in 9 parts. Paris, 1877-1919.
• DEECKE, WILHELM. Die Falisker. Strassburg, 1888.
• DEUBNER, LUDWIG. De incubatione. Giessen, 1899.
  – Lupercalia. Archiv fur Religionswissenschaft, vol. xiii, 1910. (Arch. f. Rel.)

- DIELS, HERMANN. Sibyllinische Blätter. Berlin, 1890,
- DIETERICH, ALBRECHT. De hymnis orphicis. Marburg, 1891, (Hym. orph.)
  – Eine Mithrasliturgie. Leipzig, 1910. (Mithras.)
  – Mutter Erde. Berlin, 1913.
  – Nekyia. Leipzig, 1913.
- DUSSAUD, R. Les civilisations préhelleniques. Paris, 1914.
- EVANS, SIR ARTHUR. Minoan and Mycenaean Element in Hellenic Life. Journal of Hellenic Studies, vol. xxxii, 1912. (J. H. S., xxxii)
  – Mycenaean Tree and Pillar Cult. Journal of Hellenic Studies, vol. xxi, 1901. (J. H. S.,xxi)
  – New Archaeological Lights on the Origins of Civilization in Europe. Annual Report of Smithsonian Institute, 1916. (Smith. Inst., 1916)
  – Scripta Minoa. Oxford, 1909-. (Ser. Min.)
- FARNELL, LEWIS R. Greece and Babylon. Edinburgh, 1911. (Gr. Bab.)
  – Inaugural Lecture of the Wilde Lecturer in Natural and Comparative Religion. Oxford, 1909. (N. C. R.)
  – Greek Mythology and Religion. The Year's Work in Classical Studies, 1908.
  – Sacrificial Communion. Hibbert Journal, vol. iii, 1904. (Hibbert Jour., iii)
  – The Cults of the Greek States. 5 volumes. Oxford, 1896- 1909. (Farnell)
- FICK, AUGUST. Vorgriechische Ortsnamen. Gottingen, 1905.
- FOWLER, WILLIAM WARDE. Roman Festivals. New York. 1899. (R. F.)
  – Roman Ideas of Deity. London, 1914. (Rom. Deity)
  – The Religious Experience of the Roman People. London, 1911. (R.E.)
- FRAZER, JAMES G. The Golden Bough, a Study in Magic and Religion. 12 volumes. London, 1911-15.
- FREEMAN, E. A. The History of Sicily from the Earliest Times. 4 volumes. Oxford, 1891-4.
- FRIEDLANDER, LUDWIG. Herakles. Berlin, 1907.
- GILBERT, OTTO. Geschichte und Topographie der Stadt Rom im Altertum. 3 volumes. Leipzig, 1883-90.
- GOMME, G. L. Ethnology in Folklore. London, 1892.
- GRAILLOT, H. Le culte de Cybèle mère de dieux à Rome et dans l'empire romain. Paris, 1912.
- GRANT, MADISON. The Passing of the Great Race, or The Racial Basis of European History. New York, 1918.
- GRUPPE, OTTO. Griechische Mythologie und Religionsgeschichte. Müller's Handbuch der klassischen Altertumswissenschaft. Bd. v, Abt. 2. München, 1906.
- HALL, H. R. Aegean Archaeology. London, 1915. (A. A.)
  – Ancient History of the Near East. London, 1913.(N.E.)
  – The Oldest Civilization of Greece. London and Philadelphia, 1901 (O.C.G.)

- HAMPEL, J. Neuere Studien über die Kupferzeit. Zeitschrift für Ethnologie, vol. ii, 1896.
- HARRISON, JANE E. Prolegomena to the Study of Greek Religion, Cambridge, 1908.
- HASTINGS, JAMES. Encyclopaedia of Religion and Ethics. New York, 1908. Still in course of publication.
- HAWES, C. H. and H. B. Crete, the Forerunner of Greece. London and New York, 1911.
- HEAD, BARCLAY V. Historia Nummorum, a Manual of Greek Numismatics. New Edition. Oxford, 1911.
- HENZEN, WILHELM, Acta Fratrum Arvalium. Berlin, 1874.
- HOGARTH, D. G. Aegean Religion. Hastings, Encyclopaedia of Religion and Ethics, vol. i. (Aeg. Rei.)
  – Authority and Archaeology, Sacred and Profane, London, 1899. (Auth. &Arch.)
  – The Zakro Sealings. Journal of Hellenic Studies, vol. xxii, 1902. J.H.S.,xxii)
- HUNTERIAN COLLECTION. See Macdonald, G.
- HUSCHKE, EDUARD. Das alte romische Jahr und seine Tage. Breslau, 1869.
- IMMERWAHR, WALTER. Die Kulte und Mythen Arkadiens. Leipzig, 1891.
- JEVONS, FRANK B. An Introduction to the History of Religion, London, 1914.
- JORDAN, HEINRICH. De larum imaginibus. Annali dell' Istituto, vol.xxxiii, 1862. (Lar. im.)
  – Kritische Beitrage zur Geschichte der lateinischen Sprache. Berlin, 1879. (Krit. Beitr.)
- KEANE, A. H. Man, Past and Present (revised and largely rewritten by A. H. Iniggen and A. C. Haddon). Cambridge, 1920. (M. P. P.)
  – World's Peoples. NewYork, 1908. (W.P.)
- KELLER, OTTO. Die antike Tierwelt. Leipzig, 1909. (Ant.Tier.)
  – Thieredes klassischen Altertums. 2 volumes. Innsbruch, 1887. (Thiere Kl. Alt.)
- KLAUSEN, R. H. Aeneas und die Penaten. Hamburg, 1839-40.
- KRETSCHMER, PAUL. Einleitung in die Geschichte der griechischen Sprache. Gottingen, 1896.
- LANG, ANDREW. Homer and his Age. London, 1906. (H. A.)
  – World of Homer. London and NewYork, 1910. (W.H.)
- LAWSON, JOHN C. Modern Greek Folklore and Ancient Greek Religion. Cambridge, 1910.
- LEAF, WALTER. Homer and History. London, 1915.

- LIEBRECHT, FELIX. Zur Volkskunde. Heilbronn, 1879.
- LIPPERT, JULIUS. Allgemeine Geschichte des Priestertums. 2 volumes. Berlin, 1883-4.
- LUBKERS, FRIEDRICH. Reallexikon des klassischen Altertums, Leipzig und Berlin, 1914.
- MACDONALD, GEORGE. Catalogue of Greek Coins in the Hunterian Collection. Glasgow, 1899-1905. (Hunterian Collection)
- MACKENZIE, DONALD A. Myths of Babylonia and Assyria. London, 1915. (Bab.)
  - Myths of Crete and Pre-Hellenic Europe. London, 1917. (Crete)
- MANNHARDT, W. Mythologische Forschungen. Strassburg, 1884. (Myth. Forsch.)
  - Antike Wald- und Feldkulte, Berlin, 1905. (W. F.)
- MARQUARDT, JOACHIM. Romische Staatsverwaltung. 3 volumes. Leipzig, 1885.
- MERLIN, A. L'Aventin dans l'antiquité. Paris, 1906
- MEYER, EDUARD. Geschichte des Altertums, 2 volumes. Stuttgart und Berlin, 1913.
- MODESTOV, VASILII. Introduction a l'histoire romaine (translated from the Russian by Michel Delines). Paris, 1907.
- MOMMSEN, THEODOR. Romische Forschungen. Berlin, 1864. (Rom. Forsch.)
  - History of Rome (translated from the German by W.P. Dickson). New Edition. New York, 1903-5. (H. R.)
- MONTELIUS, OSCAR. Die vorklassische Chronologie Italiens. 2 volumes. Stockholm, 1912 (Chronologie)
  - La civilisation primitive en Italie depuis l'introduction des métaux. 5 volumes. Stockholm, 1895-1910. (Montelius)
- MOSSO, ANGELO. The Dawn of Mediterranean Civilization (translated from the Italian by Marian C. Harrison). New York, 1911.
- MÜLLER, K.O. Die Etrusker (neue Bearbeitung von Wilhelm Deecke). 2 volumes. Stuttgart, 1877.
- MUNRO, R. Palaeolithic Man and the Terramara Settlements in Europe. Edinburgh, 1912.
- MURRAY, GILBERT. Four Stages of Greek Religion. New York, 1912.
- MYRES, J. L. A History of the Pelasgian Theory. Journal of Hellenic Studies, vol. xxvii, 1907.
  - Dawn of History. New York and London, 1911. (D.H.)
- NILSSON, M. P. Griechische Feste von religioser Bedeutung mit Ausschluss der attischen. Leipzig, 1906.
- OSBORN, H. F. Men of the Old Stone Age. New York, 1916.

- PAIS, ETTORE. Ancient Italy (translated from the Italian by C. D. Curtis). Chicago, 1908. (Anc. It.)
  - Ancient Legends of Roman History (translated from the Italian by Mario Cosenza). New York, 1905. (Anc. Leg.)
- PAULY-WISSOWA. Real-Encyclopädie der klassischen Altertumswissen- schaft. Stuttgart. 1894. Still in course of publication.
- PEET, THOMAS ERIC. The Stone and Bronze Ages in Italy. Oxford, 1909.
- PIGANIOL, ANDRE. Essai sur les origines de Rome. Paris, 1917.
- PINZA, GIOVANNI. Monumenti primitivi di Roma e del Lazio antico. Monumenti antichi della reale accademia dei Lincei, vol. xv, 1905. Milan. (Mon. Ant.)
  - Bullettino della commissione archeologica comunale di Roma, 1900 (Bullettino)
- POOLE, R. S. British Museum. Catalogue of Greek Coins. The Tauric Chersonese, Sarmatia, Mysia, Dacia, Thrace, etc. London, 1877.
- PRELLER, L. Romische Mythologie (bearbeitet von H. Jordan). 2 volumes. Berlin, 1881-3.
- REINACH, SALOMON. Cultes, Mythes et Religion. 4 volumes. Paris, 1905- 12. (Cultes)
  - Orpheus (translated from the French by FlorenceSimmons). London and New York, 1909.
  - Une formule orphicjue. Revue Archeologique, vol.xxxix, 1901, (Rev. Arch. xxxix)
- RHYS, SIR JOHN. Lectures on the Origin and Growth of Religion as Illus- trated by Celtic Heathendom. London, 1892.
- RIPLE Y. WILLIAM Z. The Races of Europe. New York, 1899; London, 1900.
- ROHDE, ERWIN. Psyche, Seelencult und Unsterblichkeitsglaube der Griechen. 2 volumes. Tübingen, 1907.
- ROSCHER, WILHELM H. Apollo und Mars. Leipzig, 1873.
  - Ausführliches Lexikon der griechischen und romischen Mythologie. Leipzig, 1884. Still in course of publication. (Roscher)
- SAMTER, ERNST. Die Familienfesten der Griechen und Romer. Berlin, 1901.
- DE SANCTIS, GAETANO. Storia dei Romani. 2 volumes. Milan, 1907.
- SCHRADER, OTTO. Prehistoric Antiquities of the Aryan Peoples (trans- lated from the second German edition by F. B. Jevons). London and New York, 1890.
  - Aryan Religion (Hastings, Encyclopedia of Religion, Vol. i).
  - Die Indogermanen. Leipzig, 1911.
- SCHULZE, WILHELM. Zur Geschichte lateinischer Eigennamen. Berlin, 1904.

- SCHWEGLER, A. Romische Geschichte. 3 volumes. Tübingen und Freiburg, 1870-84.
- SERGI, GIUSEPPE. The Mediterranean Race (authorized translation). London, 1901.
- SMITH, WILLIAM. Dictionary of Greek and Roman Biography and Mythology. 3 volumes. London, 1870. (Diet. Myth.)
  - Dictionary of Greek and Roman Geography. 2 volumes. London, 1870. (Diet. Geogr.)
  - A Dictionary of Greek and Roman Antiquities. 2 volumes. London, 1890. (Diet. Ant.)
- SMITH, W. ROBERTSON. The Religion of the Semites. New Edition. London, 1907. (Semites)
- STENGEL, PAUL. Die Griechischen Kultusaltertümer. Muller's Handbuch der klassischen Altertumswissenschaft, Bd. v, Abt . 3. München, 1898. (Kultusalt.)
  - Opferbrauche der Griechen. Leipzig, 1910.
- TAYLOR, ISAAC. The Origin of the Aryans. London, 1904.
- TOMASCHEK, WILHELM. Die alten Thraker. Sitzungsberichte der philosophisch-historischen Classe der kaiserlichen Akademie der Wissenschaften, Bd. cxxviii-cxxxi. Wien, 1893-4.
- TSOUNTAS, CHRESTos, and MANATT, J. IRVING. Mycenaean Age. Boston and New York,1897.
- TYLOR, E. B. Primitive Culture. London, 1903.
- UNGER, G. F. Die Lupercalien. Rheinisches Museum, vol. xxxvi, 1881.
- USENER, HERMANN. Götternamen. Bonn, 1896.
  - Milch und Honig. Rheinisches Museum, vol. lvii, 1902.
- WACE, A. J. B., and THOMPSON, M. S. Prehistoric Thessaly. Cambridge, 1912.
- WALDE, ALOIS. Lateinisches etymologisches Wörterbuch. Heidelberg, 1910.
- WESTERMARCK, EDVARD A. The Origin and Development of the Moral Ideas. 2 volumes. London, 1908-12.
- WISSOWA, GEORG. Religion und Kultus der Römer. Müller's Handbuch der klassischen Altert umswissenschaft, Bd. v, Abt. 2. München, 1912. (R. K.)
- WORSAAE, J. J. A. The Prehistory of the North (translated by H. F. M. Simpson). London, 1886.

About the author

2. Alberta Mildred Franklin

VAMzzz Publishing

Paper books

More Occult and Esoteric Books

Alberta Mildred Franklin

Alberta Mildred Franklin was born December 10, 1880, at Farmingdale, New Jersey. She was graduated from Wellesley College with the degree of Bachelor of Arts in 1904. During her course she was made a Durant Scholar. She received the degree of Master of Arts from Columbia University in 1909.

In 1904–1905 she was teacher of Latin and Greek in the High School of Atlantic Highlands, New Jersey; in 1905–1906, teacher of Latin and Ancient History in the Girls' Classical School, Pasadena, California; in 1906–1908, teacher of Latin and English in the Collegiate School, Passaic, New Jersey; in 1909–1915, teacher of Latin and Ancient History in the Barnard School for Girls, New York City; in 1915–1919, Professor of Latin and Greek at Lake Erie College, Painesville, Ohio; in 1919–1921, Associate Professor of Latin and Greek in Wilson College, Chambersburg, Pennsylvania.

During the years 1907–1914 she was studying at Columbia University under the direction of Professors Frank Frost Abbott, George Willis Botsford, John Raymond Crawford, James Chidester Egbert, Henry Rushton Fairclough, Roscoe Guernsey, Charles Knapp, Nelson Glenn McCrea, Harry Thurston Peck, Edward Delavan Perry, LaRue Van Hook and James

Rignall Wheeler. In 1921 she was appointed
Professor of Classics in Wilson College,
Chambersburg, Pennsylvania. Alberta
Mildred Franklin died September 27, 1970.

'Franklin was a Professor of Latin and ■ Greek.'

The Lupercalian Festival in Rome (ca. 1578–1610),
drawing by the circle of Adam Elsheimer, showing the Luperci dressed
as dogs and goats, with Cupid and personifications of fertility.

Recommended

*The Eleusinian and
Bacchic Mysteries*
A Dissertation
by Thomas Taylor
200 pages, Paperback
ISBN 9789492355294

The Eleusinian and Bacchic Mysteries explain a lost fundament, on which
an important part of the ancient pagan and occult tradition in Europe
was built. These mysteries once represented the spiritual life of Greece,
and were considered for two thousand years and more, the appointed
means for regeneration through an interior union with the Divine
Essence. However absurd, or even offensive or obscene, they may seem
to modern spirituality, we should be careful not to condemn what the
ancient Greek – and Romans – have esteemed holy. *The Eleusinian and
Bacchic Mysteries* focus on life, death and rebirth in the present, identical
with the living nature, which was regarded as the converging of past and
future. In this context the mystae, or initiates, learned the aporrheta, or
secret meaning of the rites, and were thenceforth denominated ephori,
or epoptæ (seers). Sacred orgies were celebrated on every fifth year; and
began on the 15th of the month Boëdromian or September.
This work offers a thrilling and invaluable body of reference and insight
to the student of the occult, as well as to academics and micro-historians
focused on the deeper layers of Greek religion.

Ophiolatreia
Rites and Mysteries of Serpent Worship
by Hargrave Jennings
186 pages, Paperback, ISBN 9789492355126

An account of the rites and mysteries connected with the origin, rise and development of serpent worship in various parts of the world, enriched with interesting traditions, and a full description of the celebrated serpent mounds & temples, the whole forming an exposition of one of the phases of phallic, or sex worship.

Amazons - *Two publications in one book* -
I. *The Amazons* by Guy Cadogan Rothery
II. *Religious Cults Associated With the Amazons*
     by Florence Mary Bennett
328 pages, Paperback, ISBN 9789492355089

Contents I: The Amazons of Antiquity – Amazons in Far Asia – Modern Amazons of the Caucasus – Amazons of Europe – Amazons of Africa – Amazons of America – The Amazon Stones. Contents II: The Amazons in Greek legend – The Great Mother – Ephesian Artemis – Artemis Astrateia and Apollo Amazonius – Ares.

Religion and Lust
or *The Physical Correlation of Religious Emotion and Sexual Desire*
by James Weir Jr.
146 pages, Paperback, ISBN 9789492355270

In *Religion and Lust,* author James Weir Jr. investigates the origins of religious feeling, the once world wide spread fertility worship and the physical correlation of religious emotion and sexual desire. A major part of the work is filled with a colourful collection of religious or semi-religious, sexual rites, once practiced all over the globe, connecting the most "primitive" tribe to the most "civilized" nations.

Voodoos and Obeahs
Phases of West India Witchcraft
by Joseph J. Williams
374 pages, Paperback, ISBN 9789492355119

This work goes into great depth concerning the New World-African connection and is highly recommended if you want a deep understanding of the dramatic historical background of Haitian and Jamaican magic and witchcraft, and the profound influence of imperialism, slavery and racism on its development. Williams includes numerous quotations from rare documents and books on the topic.

Mysteria
History of the Secret Doctrines & Mystic Rites of Ancient Religions & Medieval and Modern Secret Orders
by Dr. Otto Henne am Rhyn
288 pages, Paperback, ISBN 9789492355225

Mysteria is a treasure box of missing conspiracy links and one of the very few publications, which offer reliable information about Adam Weishaupt's Illuminati for "the web & media-disinformed". Lodge-insider Otto Henne am Rhyn takes you on a journey, back to the Mystery cults of ancient Egypt, Babylon and Greece, passes Templars and explains modern lodges.

Devil-worship in France
Or The Question of Lucifer
by Arthur Edward Waite
240 pages, Paperback, ISBN 9789492355065

In *Devil-Worship in France,* Waite attempts to discern what is genuine from what is fake in the evidence of 19th century Satanism. To get the answers he spends a great deal of time investigating the French Masonic echelon, debunking a "conspiracy of falsehood" and determining what should be understood by Satanism and what not. Huysmans' diabolical novel *Là-Bas* (1891) inspired Waite to write this sceptical analysis.